The Evidence for Jesus

Books by James D. G. Dunn
Published by The Westminster Press

The Evidence for Jesus

*Christology in the Making: A New Testament Inquiry
Into the Origins of the Doctrine of the Incarnation*

*Unity and Diversity in the New Testament: An Inquiry
Into the Character of Earliest Christianity*

Baptism in the Holy Spirit

*Jesus and the Spirit: A Study of the Religious
and Charismatic Experience of Jesus and the
First Christians as Reflected in the New Testament*

James D.G.Dunn

The Evidence for Jesus

The Westminster Press
Louisville, Kentucky 40202

First American edition

Published by The Westminster Press®
Louisville, Kentucky 40202

PRINTED IN THE UNITED STATES OF AMERICA
9 8 7 6 5 4

Library of Congress Cataloging-in-Publication Data

Dunn, James D. G., 1939–
    The evidence for Jesus.

    Bibliography: p.
    Includes index
    1. Bible. N.T. Gospels—Criticism, interpretation,
etc. 2. Jesus Christ—Historicity. 3. Jesus Christ—
Person and offices. I. Title.
BS2555.2.D86 1985   232.9′08   85-22540
ISBN 0-664-24698-2 (pbk.)

To
Kingswood Methodist Church
Nottingham

Contents

Foreword

In 1984 a British TV series from London Weekend Television created a sensation with a sequence of three programs called *Jesus: The Evidence*. The announced purpose of the series was to give viewers up-to-date information and insights on the historical evidence about Jesus: what can be known about him and how historians evaluate that evidence.

Although the series began with a balanced approach to the subject, it became increasingly provocative and controversial by inviting as experts on the subject a predominance of scholars whose views reject, or at least call into question, traditional interpretations of the evidence about Jesus. Further, there seems to have been some intention to make the public think that the scholarly majority was trying to suppress the results of new discoveries and new interpretations, since they ran counter to orthodox views. Understandably, some viewers were annoyed at having been apparently deprived of access to new and revolutionary information about Jesus, while many others were shaken by allegedly historical evidence which challenged the traditional understandings of Jesus. When the series appeared on public television in the United States, it did not create the stir here that it did in Great Britain, in part because it was not so widely seen.

British television offered a follow-up series in an attempt to give more moderate biblical scholars a chance to present their side of the case and to respond to the radicals. As a result the controversy was, if anything, extended and enlarged. Coming in conjunction with the heated debate that arose when a theologian with controversial views on the virgin birth and resurrection was consecrated a Bishop of the Church of England, thoughtful people—in and out of the churches—raised serious questions: Is the traditional faith of the church obsolete? Is the church not being honest with the public? Have such recent discoveries as the Dead Sea Scrolls and the Gnostic library in Egypt discredited the Gospel picture of Jesus as we have known it? Is the evidence not being candidly presented and discussed?

The dominant voices among the group of British and American scholars interviewed by the producers of the original British series had seemed to answer these questions in the affirmative. Fortunately, there were scholarly and churchly leaders across Great Britain who raised serious and responsible challenges to these radical conclusions. Among the latter was James D. G. Dunn, Professor of Divinity at the University of Durham in northern England, an active churchman and a prolific writer. Professor Dunn is personally interested in the daily life and faith aspects of Christianity as well as in its intellectual dimensions. It was appropriate, therefore, that the Durham Council of Churches should ask him to give a series of lectures to an interchurch audience on the same topic, "Jesus: The Evidence"—though for publication purposes the title has been given a more positive note. These lectures have been published in Great Britain and are now offered to American readers.

The author's style represents an admirable balance between careful, informed analysis of the evidence and the ability to discuss the material with a minimum of technical jargon. There is a refreshing candor in Professor Dunn's approach. He takes his lay readers seriously and introduces them in a lucid way to scholarly examination of the New Testament evidence. The result is an excellent introduction to the study of the Gospels which provides a fine base for exploring other dimensions in addition to the historical questions. There is an abundance of sound advice to the reader about what to look for and what not to look for; about how different the ancient world's approaches to biography and historical reporting are from our own; about the distinctive viewpoints presented by each of the Gospel writers; about the ancient meaning of a basic term like "Son of God" as used by and applied to Jesus.

One of the most effective sections of the book is the chapter dealing with the resurrection. What is the evidence that Jesus rose from the dead? What did the early church writers, especially Paul, mean by the claim? The author makes a powerful case for his assertion that belief in the resurrection of Jesus can be documented very soon after his death, contrary to the theory advanced by some that the idea of the resurrection was set out as a means of bolstering the eroding confidence of Jesus' followers as time passed and the world seemingly remained unchanged.

A central contribution of this book is the author's detailed sketch of some of the differences in belief, in organizational structure, and in future expectations that characterized the various groups within the early church—which was nevertheless united in its belief that God had raised Jesus from the dead. By pointing out that differing views were present in the church from earliest times, Professor Dunn warns against the modern tendency—represented by both conservative and ecumenical movements—to set up a single norm for belief or church organization. Instead, he pleads for Christians to recognize and to accept one another in spite of the diversity of faith and practice. He also demonstrates how fundamentally different Jesus was from either the founder of the Dead Sea community or from the figure of Christ represented in the various Gnostic Gospels, where he is often a kind of divine visitor masquerading as a human being. He notes how late (second to fourth century) these Gnostic Gospels are, and how they betray their having developed their ideas on the basis of the canonical Gospels. These arguments run counter to some of the sensational claims that Jesus was a Gnostic or a magician or a member of the Dead Sea sect, or that he never lived!

What Professor Dunn has written is not a simpleminded knee-jerk reaction to a serious scholarly challenge, not a know-nothing conservative retreat. Instead, these chapters are informed and informative, scholarly and devout, honest and straightforward. They should serve well for lay study groups in churches, for ministers who want to catch up with what is going on in the field of studies of Jesus, and for adult study courses, in or out of the church, on or off campus. They could also serve effectively in undergraduate religion courses as a readable, nontechnical introduction to sources and critical methods in the study of the Gospels.

This book is an attractive, readable, sensible counterbalance to sensationalism. Too much is at stake on the matter of common understanding of Jesus—at stake for the church and for contemporary culture—to allow the evidence about him to be exploited by those who for personal reasons want to discredit him or to undermine the Christian tradition. James Dunn offers here a sane, wise, readable response to the spoilers, as well as a model for serious study of the evidence.

Howard Clark Kee

Boston University

Preface

In April 1984 a London Weekend Television series entitled *Jesus: The Evidence* appeared in Britain. The object of the three-part program was to make a wider public aware of how New Testament scholars and historians of Christian origins have come to view the beginnings of Christianity. The series set itself the task of demonstrating the impact of historical scholarship on the traditional Christian understanding of who Jesus was and how he came to be regarded as God incarnate. It was an attempt to bridge the gap between the scholar's study and the pew, in order that the impact of such scholarly findings might be felt more widely.

The idea was a laudable one. Such a gap undoubtedly exists, a gap both of communication and of understanding, which gives considerable occasion for misunderstanding and confusion. Unfortunately the series served, if anything, to widen the gap rather than to span it. The opening program was on the whole a well-balanced presentation of developments behind and conclusions of current New Testament scholarship. But, regrettably, as the series progressed the presentation of Christianity's beginnings became increasingly unbalanced. Maverick and unrepresentative opinions were given more exposure in the first two programs than they probably deserved, but at least the failure of such opinions to win much (if any) support was noted, and viewpoints more typical of the bulk of scholarship were given reasonable coverage. However, in the third program all restraint seems to have been cast aside, and any attempt to present a balanced account of scholarly agreement and disagreement was abandoned in favor of a single, rather idiosyncratic viewpoint.

Not surprisingly, the series caused considerable puzzlement and even distress to many Christians—a distress which was aired on a subsequent current affairs program and a puzzlement which could not be set at rest by a discussion program following the series. A large part of the problem was that the series had mixed, in too indiscriminate a way, both the representative and the unrepresentative views of particular scholars. From what they saw and heard, viewers who lacked training in biblical studies or theology were unable to distinguish between the weightier and the less weighty opinions. They were given too little advice as to whether what was projected was accepted by the majority of scholars in this field or only by a lone voice resisting the larger consensus. Of course, scholarship does not and should not proceed by majority vote! One scholar in a hundred may be right, and the remaining ninety-nine wrong. But when lay people are being exposed to the claims of scholarship, they at least have a right to know how well these claims have been received by other scholars.

The task to which *Jesus: The Evidence* addressed itself is therefore important. Christians *should* want to know the truth—even when it hurts. But the programs failed to carry through the task to best effect. Since viewers did not know how much weight to put upon the various views expressed, there was a considerable danger that they would lump them all together and dismiss the claims of scholarship as a whole. Instead of helping to advance the education of the Christian public, the series may have set it back—may, indeed, have strengthened rather than weakened the latent anti-intellectualism that lies close to the surface of much popular religion.

Because of the puzzlement and distress caused by the series, and because of its failure to give an adequately representative portrayal of the impact of scholarship on our understanding of how Christianity began, it seemed desirable to offer an alternative portrayal. The lectures on which the following chapters are based had therefore two aims. The first was to set the record straight as to what scholarship can and does say on a number of key issues relating to Jesus and the beginnings of Christianity—to exorcize, if you like, the demon of anti-intellectualism which causes some Christians to assume that all scholarship is by nature negative and skeptical. The second was to engage in a little bit of Christian adult or continuing education—something the Christian churches in Britain have not been very good at hitherto, but for which there is an ever-increasing need, as indeed the furor resulting from the series confirmed. The write-up of the lectures follows the outlines handed out at the lectures, so that the following chapters have the same twofold aim. The title was chosen, on the suggestion of John Bowden, Editor of SCM Press, both to echo the title of the TV series and to give it an appropriately more positive note.

Jesus: The Evidence raised a goodly number of issues. It would not be practical to go into them all, in either a brief lecture series or a book. But as I viewed the programs and subsequently consulted the brief notes I made at the time, it seemed to me that there certainly were four controversial claims made by the series that deserved closer attention. These formed the individual titles of the original lectures, and I have retained them as titles of the chapters that follow.

In offering this all-too-limited exercise to a wider North American readership, it is my hope that it may make a positive contribution to theological and church education programs as well. In particular, it is my hope that here too it will serve as something of a bridge between scholars and those Christians who lack professional theological training. If I am not mistaken, suspicion and fear of scholarship is even more widespread in church circles in America than in Britain: the fear that to begin to inquire into the faith is to threaten it, that even to ask questions is to undermine it; the suspicion that theology is by its nature inimical to and subversive of faith. As will be evident from what follows, I do not share these fears and suspicions, though I can appreciate the concern. But they seem to me to be rooted in a misunderstanding of theology and to have a crippling effect on that "faith which works through love." It is my earnest hope that the following chapters will help quiet some of these suspicions and fears and remove some of these misunderstandings.

In particular, too, I am conscious of the continuing debate in the United States about the Bible and its authority within church and seminary circles—the concern that the Bible is not being given its proper place or allowed to speak with its proper authority. These are concerns I share, though often in different terms from those used by the chief protagonists. Here too I would hope that these chapters can serve as something of a bridge—on the one hand by showing how little ground some very radical opinions have, whether within the New Testament or outside it; on the other by showing that, at its best, scholarship is simply trying to hear and understand the New Testament as it really is, rather than as some dogmatic opinion says it should be. Only when the New Testament writings are properly understood on their own terms can they be properly understood in their message for today.

If this book contributes in even a small measure to such bridge-building, I will be more than content.

1 The Gospels: Fact, Fiction or What?

'For the last four hundred years New Testament scholarship has steadily eroded confidence in the historical reliability of the Bible and in the image it paints of Jesus as the Son of God.' So claimed the commentary at the beginning of the third programme in the series *Jesus: the Evidence.* This was by way of a summary of what had been said in the previous programmes. Both claims are of major importance for Christians and provide the subject and starting point for our first two chapters.

In fact the focus of the claim about 'historical reliability' had been the Gospels' portrayal of Jesus. And the question about Jesus' image as 'the Son of God' centred on the issue of how Jesus was regarded during his lifetime and how he would have regarded himself. Fortunately these are more managable proportions for single lectures or chapters of an introductory kind. It is these more limited issues with which we will deal.

Is the claim about the historical reliability of the Gospels correct? Has New Testament scholarship undermined the ordinary Christian's belief that the Gospels are historically trustworthy and accurate in what they tell about Jesus?

The answer is, Yes *and* No! Let me explain, first in summary form, and then at greater length. New Testament scholarship seeks to understand the Gospels *as* they are – to recognize *what* they are. It wants to find out the degree to which the Gospels themselves are concerned with *historical information* about Jesus, and the degree to which they present an *interpretation* of that information.

So the answer is *Yes*, in that New Testament scholars have come to recognize that interpretation *is* present in the Gospels. And where there is interpretation, there is *more* than straightforward historical information. But the answer is also *No*, in that when the Gospel writers intended to provide historical information, that information *can* be trusted as reliable. The interpretation builds upon the historical information.

That is the short answer. In the rest of the chapter I will try to explain the reasoning behind that answer in more detail.

The Task of New Testament Scholarship

It is important to underline the point, before going any further, that in reaching such a conclusion the New Testament scholar is not imposing his own prejudices (whatever they may be) on the text. The chief aim of the typical New Testament scholar is to *describe* what he sees before him in the Gospels and to achieve as full as possible an *explanation* of what he sees there. In the following pages, therefore, I will begin to sketch in the outlines of what the New Testament scholar is confronted with when he studies the Gospels and hope thereby to show why he is forced *by the Gospels themselves* to reach his 'Yes and No' conclusion. We will look at some of the features and charac-teristics of the Gospels which cause New Testament scholarship to conclude that the Gospels *are* history, but not (usually) 'simple' history. Students at university or college spend a year or more on such a study of the Gospels. So the following sketch is very rough, and we can provide only a few examples.

There are a number of basic facts with which all study of the Gospels has to reckon. I have in mind four such basic facts. The first two I need only mention. The third and particularly the fourth will reward more detailed investigation.

A Gap of Thirty to Forty Years

The Gospels were not written by Jesus himself or at his dictation. They consist at best of the recollections of what Jesus did and said during his ministry in Palestine. Jesus was put to death in the early 30s of our era. The earliest Gospel was probably not written till the late 60s. So there is a time gap between Jesus and the first Gospel – a gap of about thirty-six or thirty-nine years, possibly a little more, possibly a little less.

This gap may or may not be significant in our present inquiry. On the one hand, we should not assume that the events of Jesus' ministry and his teaching necessarily faded or became confused in the minds of the disciples who had first followed him. In societies where the *spoken* word was the chief means of communication, and where a large portion of education consisted in rote-learning, memories were better trained and almost certainly a good deal more retentive. On the other hand, we should not assume that such oral transmission had the same quality as a tape recording today, or that the teachers of such oral traditions necessarily saw such parrot-like reproduction as their sole objective. The Gospels themselves present a different picture. As we shall see.

Translation from One Language to Another

Jesus preached and taught in Aramaic, the chief common man's language in first-century Palestine. But the Gospels were all written in Greek. Anyone who is able to communicate in different languages or who has had to translate from one language to another will be very aware that *all* translation involves some degree of *interpretation*. It is often the case that there is no precise equivalent in the other language, and a choice has to be made between several words in order to translate one word of the original, or a phrase has to be used instead. You only need to compare the various modern translations of the New Testament itself to see the point.

Even more difficult is it to render idioms from one language into the different idioms of another, or to allow for the nuances which particular ideas have in the original tongue. The Salvation Army when it first moved into Paris thought to launch a French equivalent to *War Cry* under the title *Amour*, but realized just in time that Army lasses trying to sell *Amour* on the Paris boulevards were liable to create a false impression! Translators soon realize that a *literal* translation is more often than not a *poor* translation, or indeed a *wrong* translation. We have to recognize, therefore, that even the act of translating Jesus' words and first reports of Jesus' doings from Aramaic to Greek necessarily involved a significant element of interpretation.

The Parallel Gospels

Three of the Gospels obviously use *the same material* for much of the time – Matthew, Mark and Luke. We will concentrate on them in this chapter and leave John's Gospel till chapter 2.

Here is one of the things which strikes the scholar when he examines these three Gospels more closely: they have so much material in common that they can be laid out in parallel columns and looked at together. This is the simple reason why Matthew, Mark and Luke are generally known as the 'synoptic' Gospels – because they can be 'seen together' (syn-optic).

To assist them in their examination of the Synoptics, scholars make use of a *synopsis* – a book in which the Gospels have been laid out to show where the matching passages come and how close (or not so close) they are. We shall draw our illustrations from the *Synopsis* edited by B. H. Throckmorton which uses the Revised Standard Verson (RSV) English text.

The first illustration demonstrates the fact of the parallel material. The section of the Index opposite covers Matt. 13.53–18.35, Mark 5.1–9.50 and Luke 8.26–9.50. If we focus attention first on the three columns in bold type on the left, it will immediately be seen that of the 31 sections (106–136) no less than 24 have two or three versions, and only 7 sections appear in a single Gospel. But this is only the parallel material which comes in the same order in each Gospel. When we include also the material in the right-hand columns (Parallels and Doublets), we will see at once that there is much more common material, and that only occasionally is there a single version without parallel (as in Mark 8.22–26). In point of fact, almost all of Mark's Gospel appears also in Matthew.

When scholars have looked more closely at particular parallel passages, the next most obvious feature has usually been *the closeness of the parallels*. Consider, for example, the section on John the Baptist's preaching common to Matthew and Luke.

JOHN'S PREACHING OF REPENTANCE

Matt. 3.7–10	Luke 3.7–9
[7] But when he saw many of the Pharisees and Saducees coming for baptism, he said to them, 'You brood of vipers! Who warned you to flee from the wrath to come? [8] Bear fruit that befits repentance, [9] and do not presume to say to yourselves, "We have Abraham as our father"; for I tell you, God is able from these stones to raise up children to Abraham. [10] Even now the axe is laid to the root of the trees; every tree therefore that does not bear good fruit is cut down and thrown into the fire.'	[7] He said therefore to the multitudes that came out to be baptized by him, 'You brood of vipers! Who warned you to flee from the wrath to come? [8] Bear fruits that befit repentance, and do not begin to say to yourselves, "We have Abraham as our father"; for I tell you, God is able from these stones to raise up children to Abraham. [9] Even now the axe is laid to the root of the trees; every tree therefore that does not bear good fruit is cut down and thrown into the fire.'

Here there is almost one hundred per cent verbal agreement in the two accounts of the Baptist's words, as the underlining makes clear.

Or consider the account of Jesus healing in the synagogue at Capernaum common to Mark and Luke.

INDEX OF THE GOSPEL PARALLELS

	Matt.	Mark	Luke	Parallels and Doublets Matt.	Mark	Luke
106 The Gerasene Demoniac	—	5. 1–20	26–39	8.28–34		
107 Jairus' Daughter and a Woman's Faith	—	21–43	40–56	9.18–26		
108 Jesus is Rejected at Nazareth	13. 53–58	6. 1–6a	—			*4.16–30*
109 The Sending out of the Twelve	—	6b–13	9.1–6	9.35 10.1, 9–11, 14	3.14–15	*10.1–12*
110 Herod Thinks Jesus is John, Risen	14.1–2	14–16	7–9			
111 The Death of John	3–12	17–29	—			*3.19–20*
112 The Return of the Twelve, and the Feeding of the Five Thousand	13–21	30–44	10–17	9.36 *15.32–39*	*8.1–10*	10.17
113 The Walking on the Water	22–33	45–52	—			
114 Healings at Gennesaret	34–36	53–56	—	4.24	*1.32 f.* 3.10	*4.40 f.* 6.18–19 6.39
115 What Defiles a Man	15.1–20	7.1–23	—			
116 The Syrophoenician Woman	21–28	24–30	—			
117 The Healing of Many Sick Persons – of the Deaf Mute	15.29–31	7.31–37	—			
118 The Feeding of the Four Thousand	32–39	8.1–10	—	*14.13–21*	*6.30–44*	*9.10–17*
119 The Pharisees Seek a Sign	16.1–4	11–13	—	12.38–39		11.16, 29 12.54–56
120 A Discourse on Leaven	5–12	14–21	—			12.1
121 The Blind Man of Bethsaida	—	22–26	—			
122 The Confession at Caesarea Philippi and the First Prediction of the Passion	13–23	27–33	9.18–22	18.18		
123 The Conditions of Discipleship	24–28	34–9.1	23–27	10.33, 38–39		12.9 14.27 17.33
124 The Transfiguration	17.1–8	9.2–8	28–36			
125 The Coming of Elijah	9–13	9–13	—			*9.37*
126 An Epileptic Boy Healed	14–21	14–29	37–43a	*17.9* 21.21	9.9 11.22–23	17.6
127 The Second Prediction of the Passion	22–23	30–32	43b–45			
128 The Temple Tax	24–27	—	—			
129 The Dispute about Greatness	18.1–5	33–37	46–48	10.40 20.26–27 23.11–12	10.15, 43–44	*10.16* 14.11 18.14, 17 22.26
130 The Strange Exorcist	—	38–41	49–50	10.42 12.30		11.23
131 On Temptations	6–9	42–48	—	5.29–30		17.1–2
132 Concerning Salt	—	49–50	—	5.13		14.34–35
133 The Lost Sheep	10–14	—	—			15.3–7
134 On Reproving One's Brother	15–20	—	—	16.19		17.3
135 On Reconciliation	21–22	—	—			17.4
136 The Parable of the Unmerciful Servant	23–35	—	—	6.15		

JESUS IN THE SYNAGOGUE AT CAPERNAUM

Matt. 7.28–29	Mark 1.21–28	Luke 4.31–37

²¹ And they went into Caper-naum; and **immediately** on the sabbath he entered the synagogue and taught. ²² And they were astonished at his teaching, for he taught them as one who had authority, and not as the scribes.

²³ And **immediately** there was in their synagogue a man with an unclean spirit; ²⁴ and he cried out,

²⁸ And when Jesus finished these saying, the crowds were astonished at his teaching, ²⁹ for he taught them as one who had authority, and not as their scribes.

³¹ And he went down to Caper-naum, a city of Galilee. And he was teaching them on the sabbath; ³² and they were astonished at his teaching, for his word was with authority.

³³ And in the synagogue there was a man who had the spirit of an unclean demon; and he cried out with a loud voice, ³⁴ 'Ah! What have you to do with us, Jesus of Nazareth? Have you come to destroy us? I know who you are, the Holy One of God.' ³⁵ But Jesus rebuked him, saying, 'Be silent, and come out of him!' And when the demon had thrown him down in the midst, he came out of him, having done him no harm. ³⁶ And they were all amazed and said to one another, 'What is this word? For with authority and power he commands the unclean spirits, and they come out.' ³⁷ And reports of him went out into every place in the surrounding region.

'What have you to do with us, Jesus of Nazareth? Have you come to destroy us? I know who you are, the Holy One of God.' ²⁵ But Jesus rebuked him, saying, 'Be silent, and come out of him!' ²⁶ And the unclean spirit, convulsing him and crying with a loud voice, came out of him. ²⁷ And they were all amazed, so that they questioned among themselves, saying, 'What is this? A new teaching! With authority he commands even the unclean spirits, and they obey him.' ²⁸ And at once his fame spread everywhere through-out all the surrounding region of Galilee.

Here the verbal agreement is not so close, but still close enough to put it beyond doubt that we are dealing with the same episode. It is probably significant that the parallel becomes closest in the verbal exchange between the demoniac and Jesus (Mark, verses 24–25; Luke, verses 34–35) – a strong indication that this was seen as the focal point of the story. We might also note in passing the repeated 'immediately', 'immediately', 'at once' of Mark 1.21, 23, 28 – a feature of Mark's style which has the effect of keeping the narrative lively and on the move.

A third example is the account of Jesus' rejection at Nazareth, where the parallel this time is particularly between Matthew and Mark.

JESUS IS REJECTED AT NAZARETH

Matt 13.53–58   Mark 6.1–6a

⁵³ And when Jesus had finished these parables, he went away from there, ⁵⁴ and coming to his own country he taught them in their synagogue, so that they were astonished, and said,"Where did this man get this wisdom and these mighty works? ⁵⁵ Is not this the carpenter's son? Is not his mother called Mary? And are not his brothers James and Joseph and Simon and Judas? ⁵⁶ And are not all his sisters with us? Where then did this man get all this?' ⁵⁷ And they took offense at him. But Jesus said to them, "A prophet is not without honor except in his own country and in his own house.' ⁵⁸ And he did not do many mighty works there, because of their unbelief.	¹ He went away from there and came to his own country; and his disciples followed him. ² And on the sabbath he began to teach in the synagogue; and many who heard him were astonished, saying, 'Where did this man get all this? What is the wisdom given to him? What mighty works are wrought by his hands! ³ Is not this the carpenter, the son of Mary and brother of James and Joses and Judas and Simon, and are not his sisters here with us?' And they took offense at him. ⁴ And Jesus said to them, "A prophet is not without honor, except in his own country, and among his own kin, and in his own house.' ⁵ And he could do no mighty work there, except that he laid his hands upon a few sick people and healed them. ⁶ And he marveled because of their unbelief.

Once again the parallel is so close that we must obviously be dealing with the same tradition.

Such closeness between accounts in different Gospels can only be explained if in each case the Gospels are using *the very same material*. Either the particular evangelist knew one of the other Gospels and drew the material he wanted directly from there. Or both evangelists had a common source on which they drew independently of each other.

Moreover, these traditions about Jesus were already in *Greek* before they reached the evangelists. We can tell this because the verbal agreement is so close. Whereas, if each evangelist had been translating independently from a common *Aramaic* source the *Greek* translations would certainly have diverged from each other to a much greater extent.

The fact that the *same* Greek translations of the earliest accounts of Jesus (in Aramaic) were so influential, providing a major part of two (or all three) of the evangelist's material, is a strong indication that the traditions about Jesus, as they circulated among the earliest churches and were used by them (in worship and evangelism, instruction and apologetic), took a well known and well established form.

This suggests a strong continuity between the earliest stages of the tradition and the tradition as we now have it in the Gospels themselves. And where the continuity between the first eye- and ear-witnesses is so strong, the likelihood that we are confronted with a solid base of *historical information* is immeasurably strengthened.

Tradition Edited and Interpreted

However, it is also important to realize that the evangelists were not simply recorders of tradition. They were also editors. They worked upon and *interpreted* the traditions they used. This is the point at which the original claim made by *Jesus: the Evidence* about New Testament scholarship begins to gain some substance. So it is worth developing this aspect of the Gospel traditions with some care. And the simplest way to do that is to document and illustrate the kind of features which have caught the scholar's eye when he goes into more detailed examination of the synoptic parallels.

Different combinations

The evangelists put the traditions about Jesus together *in different ways*. For example, the Sermon on the Mount, set out opposite.

In the first column headed Matt. we see the familiar divisions of the Sermon in Matt. 5–7. But in the right-hand column (Luke), notice how and where the parallels come – from chapters 6, 8, 11, 14, 16, 12, 16, 6, 11, etc. – *not* in connected order. How to explain this feature? It is unlikely that Luke has broken up and scattered a single connected sermon. The most obvious explanation for what we see before us is rather that Matthew *constructed* the Sermon by grouping together elements of Jesus' teaching which had come from *different* points in his ministry. In other words the Sermon on the Mount was almost certainly never delivered by Jesus as a complete sermon. It is simply an editorial device to hold together a range of similar and closely related teaching material derived from Jesus. It follows that the impression given by Matthew that the sermon was delivered on a single occasion is in fact *not historical*. But neither was it intended to be! The technique of setting Jesus' teaching in such a typical framework would have been a quite familiar and acceptable editorial device. The (strictly speaking) historical unreliability of the *framework* leaves the question of the historical reliability of the *content* quite unaffected.

This conclusion, which follows from the internal evidence of the Gospels themselves, has an interesting confirmation from evidence

THE SERMON ON THE MOUNT: MATTHEW 5–7

		Matt.	Mark	Luke	Parallels and Doublets Matt.	Mark	Luke
18	Introduction	5. 1–2	—	—	*3.13*		6.12, 20
19	The Beatitudes	3–12	—	—			6.20–23
20	The Parables of Salt and Light	13–16	—	—		4.21 9.50	8.16 11.33 14.34–35
21	Words of Jesus on the Law	17–20	—	—	*24.35*	*13.31*	16.17 *21.33*
22	On Murder	21–26	—	—			12.57–59
23	On Adultery	27–30	—	—	18.8–9	9.43–48	
24	On Divorce	31–32	—	—	19.9	10.11, 12	16.18
25	On Swearing	33–37	—	—	*23.16–22*		
26	On Retaliation	38–42	—	—			6.29–30
27	On Love of One's Enemies	43–48	—	—			6.27–28, 32–36
28	On Almsgiving	6. 1–4	—	—			
29	On Prayer	5–8	—	—			
30	The Lord's Prayer	9–15	—	—	*18.35*	11.25 [26]	11.2–4
31	Words of Jesus on Fasting	16–18	—	—			
32	On Treasures	19–21	—	—			12.33–34
33	The Sound Eye	22–23	—	—			11.34–36
34	Words of Jesus on Serving Two Masters	24	—	—			16.13
35	On Anxiety	25–34	—	—			12.22–31
36	On Judging	7. 1–5	—	—		4.24	6.37–38, 41–42
37	On Profaning the Holy	6	—	—			
38	God's Answering of Prayer	7–11	—	—			11.9–13
39	'The Golden Rule'	12	—	—			6.31
40	The Narrow Gate	13–14	—	—			13.23–24
41	The Test of a Good Man	15–20	—	—	*3.10* 12.33–35		*3.9* 6.43–45
42	Warning against Self-Deception	21–23	—	—			6.46 13.26–27
43	Hearers and Doers of the Word	24–27	—	—			6.47–49
44	The End of the Sermon	28–29	—	—		1.21, 22	4.31–32 *7.1 a*

outside the Gospels. Papias, a Christian writer from the second century, in describing the Gospel of Mark, reports that

> Mark, who was the interpreter of Peter, wrote down accurately all that he remembered . . . but not in order. . . . he accompanied Peter, who adapted his instruction as necessity required (Eusebius, *Ecclesiastical History* 3.39).

Here is a further reminder that we cannot and should not assume that the evangelists were attempting to produce what *we* would call a biography of Jesus. Their concern was rather to present their

material in the way which best served their evangelistic, apologetic
or teaching purposes. Clearly they were concerned to preserve the
memory of Jesus' words and deeds. But, equally clearly, they were
not concerned to reproduce these accounts in the order in which they
happened.

Different lengths

The evangelists tell their stories in *longer and shorter versions*.
Consider, for example, the account of the disciples plucking ears of
grain on the Sabbath.

PLUCKING EARS OF GRAIN ON THE SABBATH

Matt. 12.1–8	Mark 2.23–28	Luke 6.1–5
¹ At that time Jesus went through the grainfields on the sabbath; his disciples were hungry, and they began to pluck ears of grain and to eat. ² But when the Pharisees saw it, they said to him, "Look, your disciples are doing what is not lawful to do on the sabbath.' ³ He said to them, 'Have you not read what David did, when he was hungry, and those who were with him: ⁴ how he entered the house of God	²³ One sabbath he was going through the grainfields; and as they made their way his disciples began to pluck ears of grain. ²⁴ And the Pharisees said to him, 'Look, why are they doing what is not lawful on the sabbath?' ²⁵ And he said to them, 'Have you never read what David did, when he was in need and was hungry, he and those who were with him: ²⁶ how he entered the house of God, when Abiathar was high priest, and ate the bread	¹ On a sabbath, while he was going through the grainfields, his disciples plucked and ate some ears of grain, rubbing them in their hands. ² But some of the Pharisees said, 'Why are you doing what is not lawful to do on the sabbath?' ³ And Jesus answered, 'Have you not read what David did when he was hungry, he and those who were with him: ⁴ how he entered the house of God,
and ate the bread of the Presence, which it was not lawful for him to eat nor for those who were with him, but only for the priests? ⁵ Or have you not read in the law how on the sabbath the priests in the temple profane the sabbath, and are guiltless? ⁶ I tell you, something greater than the temple is here. ⁷ And if you had known what this means, 'I desire mercy, and not sacrifice,' you would not have condemned the guiltless.	of the Presence, which it is not lawful for any but the priests to eat, and also gave it to those who were with him?'	and took and ate the bread of the Presence, which it is not lawful for any but the priests to eat, and also gave it to those with him?'
	²⁷ And he said to them, 'The sabbath was made for man, not man for the sabbath; ²⁸ so the	⁵ And he said to them,
⁸ For the Son of man is lord of the sabbath.'	Son of man is lord even of the sabbath.'	'The Son of man is lord of the sabbath.'

The most obvious difference is the longer version of Matthew – by virtue of his having three extra verses (vv.5–7). The argument used by Jesus in these verses fits more closely to the central issue of the dispute ('doing what is not lawful on the sabbath'). So it is less likely that Mark's version left just that section out of a larger version; and more likely that Matthew inserted it (from where we do not know) in order to tie Jesus' answer more closely to the issue. But one way or other, the tradition of the episode has been either expanded or contracted in the course of transmission.

On the other hand, both Matthew and Luke lack a parallel to v. 27 of Mark. So again we have to conclude that those who passed on the tradition of what Jesus said in relation to the sabbath felt free to present it in a fuller or a less full version.

One other point from this passage is worth noting in passing. In v. 26, Mark's version dates David's action at the time 'when Abiathar was high priest'. This is factually inaccurate (the high priest was Ahimelech – see I Sam. 21.1). It is obviously for this reason that Matthew and Luke have both omitted the clause (as also various manuscripts of Mark itself). In this case we have to conclude either that Jesus himself was factually inaccurate or that Mark in reproducing the tradition was not concerned to present historical information with pedantic accuracy, and/or that Matthew and Luke in abbreviating a word of Jesus also felt free to act as more than mere passers on of tradition.

A better example of longer and shorter versions are the three accounts of the raising of Jairus' daughter and the healing of the woman with internal bleeding.

JAIRUS' DAUGHTER AND A WOMAN'S FAITH

Matt. 9.18–26	Mark 5.21–43	Luke 8.40–56
	21 And when Jesus had crossed again in the boat to the other side, a great crowd gathered about him; and he was beside the sea. 22 Then came one of the rulers of the synagogue, Jairus by name; and seeing him, he fell at his feet, 23 and besought him, saying, 'My little daughter is at the point of death. Come and lay your hands on her, so that she may be made well, and live.' 24 And he went with him. And a great crowd followed him and pressed round him.	40 Now when Jesus returned, the crowd welcomed him, for they were all waiting for him. 41 And there came a man named Jairus, who was a ruler of the synagogue; and falling at Jesus' feet he besought him to come to his house, 42 for he had an only daughter, about twelve years of age, and she was dying. As he went, the people pressed round him.
18 While he was thus speaking to them, behold, a ruler came in and knelt before him, saying, 'My daughter has just died; but come and lay your hand on her, and she will live.' 19 And Jesus rose and followed him, with his disciples.		

20 And behold, a woman who had suffered from a hemorrhage for twelve years

25 And there was a woman who had had a flow of blood for twelve years, 26 and who had suffered much under many physicians, and had spent all that she had, and was no better but rather grew worse. 27 She had heard the reports about Jesus,

43 And a woman who had had a flow of blood for twelve years and could not be healed by any one,

came up behind him and touched the fringe of his garment. 24 For she said to herself, 'If I only touch his garment, I shall be made well.'

and came up behind him in the crowd and touched his garment. 28 For she said, 'If I touch even his garments, I shall be made well.' 29 And immediately the hemorrhage ceased; and she felt in her body that she was healed of her disease. 30 And Jesus, perceiving in himself that power had gone forth from him, immediately turned about in the crowd, and said, 'Who touched my garments?'31 And his disciples said to him, 'You see the crowd pressing around you, and yet you say, "Who touched me?" ' 32 And he looked around to see who had done it. 33 But the woman, knowing what had been done to her, came in fear and trembling and fell down before him, and told him the whole truth.

44 came up behind him, and touched the fringe of his garment;

and immediately her flow of blood ceased.

45 And Jesus said, 'Who was it that touched me?' When all denied it, Peter said, 'Master, the multitudes surround you and press upon you!' 46 But Jesus said, 'Some one touched me; for I perceive that power has gone forth from me.'

47 And when the woman saw that she was not hidden, she came trembling, and falling down before him declared in the presence of all the people why she had touched him, and how she had been immediately healed.

22 Jesus turned, and seeing her he said, 'Take heart, daughter; your faith has made you well.' And instantly the woman was made well.

34 And he said to her, 'Daughter, your faith has made you well; go in peace, and be healed of your disease.'
35 While he was still speaking, there came from the ruler's house some who said, 'Your daughter is dead. Why trouble the Teacher any further? 36 But ignoring what they said, Jesus said to the ruler of the synagogue, 'Do not fear, only believe.' 37 And he allowed no one to follow him except Peter and James and John the brother

48 And he said to her, 'Daughter, your faith has made you well; go in peace.'

49 While he was still speaking, a man from the ruler's house came and said, 'Your daughter is dead; do not trouble the Teacher any more.' 50 But Jesus on hearing this answered him,

'Do not fear; only believe, and she shall be well.' 51 And when he came to the house, he permitted no one to

23 And when Jesus came to the ruler's house, and saw the flute players, and the crowd making a tumult, 24 he said,

'Depart; for the girl is not dead but sleeping.' And they laughed at him. 25 But when the crowd had been put outside,

he went in and took her by the hand,

and the girl arose.

26 And the report of this went through all that district.

of James. 38 When they came to the house of the ruler of the synagogue, he saw a tumult, and people weeping and wailing loudly. 39 And when he had entered, he said to them, 'Why do you make a tumult and weep? The child is not dead but sleeping.' 40 And they laughed at him. But he put them all outside, and took the child's father and mother and those who were with him, and went in where the child was. 41 Taking her by the hand he said to her, 'Talitha cumi'; which means, 'Little girl, I say to you, arise.' 42 And immediately the girl got up and walked; for she was twelve years old. And immediately they were overcome with amazement. 43 And he strictly charged them that no one should know this, and told them to give her something to eat.

enter with him, except Peter and John and James, and the father and mother of the child. 52 And all were weeping and bewailing her; but he said,

'Do not weep; for she is not dead but sleeping.' 53 And they laughed at him, knowing that she was dead.

54 But taking her by the hand he called, saying, 'Child, arise.' 55 And her spirit returned, and she got up at once; and he directed that something should be given her to eat. 56 And her parents were amazed; but he charged them to tell no one what had happened.

A glance is sufficient to show that Mark is significantly longer than either Matthew or Luke, and that Matthew is a good deal shorter than the others. In fact, whereas Mark uses 374 words to tell the tale, Luke uses 280 words, and Matthew only 138 words – almost two-thirds less than Mark. Again the evidence of the Gospels themselves forces us to recognize, either that one evangelist has abbreviated a fuller account of the episode, or that another has elaborated a briefer account, or both.

From both these examples we can hardly fail to conclude that the evangelists were *not* concerned merely to reproduce the stories about Jesus, and were certainly *not* concerned to reproduce with parrot-like precision or in the same detail. At the same time, it would be perverse to conclude that they were dealing with *different* episodes. Clearly it is the same story in each case, and in each case we have no reason to doubt that the story derives from memories of Jesus' ministry. But the fact remains that the story was retold in different ways, and evidently it was quite acceptable to do so.

Different emphases

The evangelists tell stories from *different angles*, to make *different points*. Consider, for example, the account of the healing of the centurion's servant.

THE CENTURION'S SERVANT

Matt. 8.5–13   Luke 7.1–10

[5] As he entered Capernaum, a centurion came forward to him, beseeching him [6] and saying, 'Lord, my servant is lying paralyzed at home, in terrible distress.' [7] And he said to him, 'I will come and heal him.'

[1] After he had ended all his sayings in the hearing of the people he entered Capernaum. [2] Now a centurion had a slave who was dear to him, who was sick and at the point of death. [3] When he heard of Jesus, **he sent to him elders** of the Jews, asking him to come and heal his slave. [4] And when they came to Jesus, they besought him earnestly, saying, '**He is worthy** to have you do this for him, [5] for he loves our nation, and he built us our synagogue.'

[8] But the centurion answered him,
'Lord,
I am not worthy to have you come under my roof;
but only say the word, and my servant will be healed. [9] For I am a man under authority, with soldiers under me; and I say to one, "'Go," and he goes, and to another, "'Come," and he comes, and to my slave, "'Do this," and he does it.' [10] When Jesus heard him, he marveled, and   said to those who followed him, '**Truly I say to you, not even in Israel have I found such faith.**
[11] 'I tell you, many will come from east and west and sit at table with
Abraham, Isaac, and Jacob
in the kingdom of heaven, [12] while the sons of the kingdom will be thrown into the outer darkness; there men will weep and gnash their teeth.'

[6] And Jesus went with them. When he was not far from the house, the centurion **sent friends to** him, saying to him, 'Lord do not trouble yourself, for **I am not worthy** to have you come under my roof; [7] **therefore I did not presume to come to you.** But say the word, and let my servant be healed. [8] For I am a man set under authority, with soldiers under me: and I say to one, "'Go," and he goes; and to another, "'Come," and he comes; and to my slave, "'Do this," and he does it.' [9] When Jesus heard this he marveled at him, and turned and said to the multitude that followed him, 'I tell you, not even in Israel have I found such faith.'
13.28–30: [28] 'There you will weep and gnash your teeth, when you see Abraham and Isaac and Jacob and all the prophets in the kingdom of God and you yourselves thrust out. [29] And men will come from east and west, and from north and south, and sit at table in the kingdom of God. [30] And behold, some are last who will be first, and some are first who will be last.'

[13] And to the centurion Jesus said, 'Go; be it done for you **as you have believed.**' And the servant was healed at that very moment.

7.10 And when **those who had been sent** returned to the house, they found the slave well.

Notice first of all that the core of the story is the same, almost word for word. As with the example above (p. 6), it looks as though the exchange between the chief characters in the episode (Jesus and the centurion) is the focal point of the story (Matt. 8.8–10; Luke 7.6b–9). With such closeness of parallel it is hardly possible to argue that there are two separate episodes here.

But notice secondly that there is nothing like the same closeness between Matthew and Luke in the lead-up to the central exchange. In fact the only points of contact between the two narratives are the mention of Jesus entering Capernaum and 'a centurion'. For the rest they differ quite markedly. In the case of Matthew the centurion himself approaches Jesus personally. In the case of Luke he sends others to speak for him. Such a difference can be explained, of course, by the fact that Matthew has chosen to abbreviate a fuller account and so to omit what he regarded as secondary detail, or at least detail of less immediate importance to the story. But whatever the reason the conclusion drawn above (p. 13) is confirmed: one or other, or both, of the evangelists were not so concerned with these details of the story; they evidently did not see it to be their task to tell the story precisely as it happened. To be sure, the divergence does not affect the central part of the story (the exchange between Jesus and the centurion), but it does mean that we today cannot be precisely sure of the detail of whether Jesus and the centurion made their exchange face to face or not.

When we look more closely at the other distinctive features of the two versions of the story the reason for these different features begins to become clearer. The reason why the accounts diverge so much is because each evangelist is trying to make a *different* point.

Matthew evidently wants to emphasize the importance of *faith*. So it is Jesus' commendation of the centurion's faith (v.10) on which he builds his account. Hence he makes a point of re-emphasizing Jesus' commendation of the centurion's faith at the end of the narrative (v.13). This also explains why he has attached Jesus' saying about membership of the kingdom at this point (vv.11–12); whereas Luke records it in a quite different context (Luke 13.28–30), indicating that most likely Jesus made the remark on some other occasion. But Matthew has chosen to insert it here, between the two commendations of the Gentile centurion's faith, so that his readers will take the very important point that entrance into the kingdom is through faith. Since it is through faith, it is open to Gentiles as well as Jews. Whereas Jews who presume upon their privileged position as God's chosen people ('the sons of the kingdom') will find themselves outside! And since the point being made focusses so strongly on the centurion's faith, it makes more sense to present an abbreviated introduction to the encounter between Jesus and the centurion in which the immediacy and directness of his faith in Jesus' authority and power comes to the fore.

On the other hand, Luke seems more concerned to emphasize the centurion's *humility*. So the element in the common core on which Luke focusses attention is the opening utterance of the centurion, 'I am not worthy' (v.6). It is for this reason that Luke has a fuller build up to the central section. For the refusal of the centurion to come in person is precisely what underscores the centurion's humility. Hence the distinctive Lukan element within the central core: 'I am not worthy . . . *therefore I did not presume to come to you*' (v.7a). The earlier mission of the elders on behalf of the centurion (vv.3–5) highlights the same point by way of contrast. Whereas the centurion says, 'I am not worthy', the elders insist, 'He is worthy' (v.4).

Here again, then, simply by observing what the evangelists actually wrote, we can see how one or other or both was willing to adapt the detail of the common tradition in order to make his own point. The editorial technique is not dissimilar to the telling of a punch-line joke. What matters in a punch-line joke is, naturally enough, the punch-line. Most retellers of such jokes know well that they must take great care to get the punch-line just right in content and timing. The build up to the punch-line is a different matter: it can be long or short; it can vary in detail, often quite considerably. So somewhat similarly with this example of a story about Jesus. Matthew and Luke recall the common core with great care, because it was on the basis of this central element that they were to build the particular point they each wanted to make (the identification of the one commended by Jesus as a *Gentile* is also part of the core). For most of the other elements of the story the evangelists show themselves to be very flexible. From this we may fairly deduce both that the common core derives from Jesus' ministry (that is why the evangelists are concerned both to reproduce it and to draw important conclusions from it) *and* that the evangelists felt free-er in their handling of what they regarded as the subsidiary detail of the story.

One of the best examples of the same story told in different versions, with different details and for different purposes, comes from outside the Gospels. In the Acts of the Apostles, written by the author of the third Gospel (Luke), we have no less than three accounts of Paul's conversion – Acts 9, 22 and 26. We need not reproduce them here, though they could quite easily be set out synoptically, side by side. When we do compare them, precisely the same features become evident as those we have observed in the story of the centurion's humility/faith.

On the one hand, the same core is present in each – again, significantly, the snatch of dialogue between Paul and the risen Christ, and again word for word (Acts 9.5–6; 22.7–10; 26.14–16).

'Saul, Saul, why do you persecute me?'
'Who are you, Lord?'
'I am Jesus, whom you are persecuting; . . . Rise . . .'.

On the other hand, the surrounding details vary a good deal. For example, in chapter 9 Paul's commissioning to take the gospel to the Gentiles is referred to only in the summons of Ananias to minister to Paul (9.15–16). In chapter 22 Ananias alludes to it when he speaks to Paul, but the more explicit commissioning seems to come later, in Jerusalem (22.15, 21). While in chapter 26 the commissioning comes immediately in the initial revelation of Jesus to Paul, and Ananias is given no mention (26.16–18).

Not least of interest in this case is the fact that it is the *same* author who tells these three *different* versions of the one story. When different authors tell different versions of the same story it is always open to us to argue that that was the version they received and they each knew no other. But in this case that argument simply will not work. In this case it is the same author (Luke) who records the different versions within the same book. That must certainly indicate that Luke himself was not concerned with pedantic uniformity or strict consistency of historical detail. On the contrary he was quite content to record three different versions whose details do not fully accord with each other. (For another example, compare 9.7 with 22.9.)

From this we may make the same deduction as in the previous example. On the one hand, the fact of the same common core, preserved constantly in the midst of such shifting variation in other details, points strongly to the conclusion that the snatch of dialogue between Paul and the one he encountered had been firmly fixed from the first – presumably burnt into Paul's own memory in the encounter itself. Common too is the element of Paul's being called by the risen Christ to take the gospel to the Gentiles. But this latter element could be and was expressed differently. The sense of commissioning, to which Paul himself bears testimony in his own letters (particularly Gal. 1.15–16), evidently did not take a fixed form in the retelling. The other details were subsidiary to these central points and could be omitted, included, or varied, presumably as the situation and the mood of the occasion determined.

In these two examples, then, we see clear cases of a core of *historical information* obviously regarded as of central importance, but also of *interpretative* use of that common core, resulting overall

in the pattern of parallel and difference which makes up our Synoptic
Gospels.

Corrections

The evangelists *correct* misleading impressions given in the earlier
versions. The key word here is 'correct'. It is not simply a case of
two versions which differ because of the evangelists' differing
emphases. There are various occasions when they go out of their way
to modify or change the earlier version. Two of the best examples
come in passages where Matthew parallels Mark and where the most
obvious explanation of the divergence between them is that Mark is
the earlier and that Matthew has introduced the divergence as a form
of correction or improvement.

The first example comes in a passage already looked at – the
rejection of Jesus at Nazareth.

JESUS IS REJECTED AT NAZARETH

Matt. 13.53–58	Mark 6.1–6a
⁵³ And when Jesus had finished these parables, he went away from there, ⁵⁴ and coming to his own country he taught them in their synagogue, so that they were astonished, and said, 'Where did this man get this wisdom and these mighty works? ⁵⁵ Is not this the **carpenter's son? Is not his mother called Mary?** And are not his brothers James and Joseph and Simon and Judas? ⁵⁶ And are not all his sisters with us? Where then did this man get all this?' ⁵⁷ And they took offense at him. But Jesus said to them, 'A prophet is not without honor except in his own country and in his own house.' ⁵⁸ And he **did not do many mighty works** there, because of their unbelief.	¹ He went away from there and came to his own country; and his disciples followed him. ² And on the sabbath he began to teach in the synagogue; and many who heard him were astonished, saying, 'Where did this man get all this? What is the wisdom given to him? What mighty works are wrought by his hands! ³ Is not this the **carpenter,** **the son** of **Mary** and brother of James and Joses and Judas and Simon, and are not his sisters here with us?' And they took offense at him. ⁴ And Jesus said to them, 'A prophet is not without honor, except in his own country, and among his own kin, and in his own house.' ⁵ And he **could do no mighty work** there, except that he laid his hands upon a few sick people and healed them. ⁶ And he marveled because of their unbelief.

We saw above (p. 6) how closely parallel the two accounts are.
This time we look at the differences. The most significant difference
comes at the end – in v.5 of Mark and v.58 of Matthew.

Mark – 'he *could* do *no* mighty work there . . .'
Matt. – 'he *did* not do *many* mighty works there'.

Mark's is the most striking version, and one can readily see that it might well have been a cause of some questioning or even of offence among some early disciples – the idea that Jesus was powerless in the face of unbelief and unable to do any miracle. Presumably this is the reason why Matthew modified Mark's account at this point; (the alternative suggestion that Mark introduced the more difficult reading by changing Matthew's version seems a good deal less likely). His abbreviation of Mark's three lines is rather neat: he keeps the *form* of Mark's first line, but alters it to convey the *sense* of the last two lines. So in fact he repeats Mark's point, but at the same time he effectively eliminates the potential problem raised by Mark's wording.

Before moving on to our next example, we should notice the other significant difference between the two accounts – Mark's v.3 and Matthew's v.55.

Mark – 'Is not this the carpenter, the son of Mary . . . ?'
Matt. – 'Is not this the carpenter's son? Is not his mother called Mary?'

In Mark Jesus himself is called 'the carpenter'. Whereas in Matthew it is not Jesus who is called the carpenter but his father. The reason for the change here lies probably in the following phrase – 'the son of Mary'. In those days a man would normally be known by reference to his father – X, son of Y. To call a man the son of his *mother* would usually imply therefore that his father was unknown – that is to say, he was illegitimate. Mark's version may, of course, provide an interesting reflection of the fact that there *was* something odd about Jesus' birth (cf. Matt. 1–2 and Luke 1–2). But the point here is that Matthew seems to have been unwilling to preserve what, in everyday language, would normally be regarded as an insult. (To call someone a 'bastard' is normally an insult in any language.)

What is also interesting is the way in which Matthew effects the change. Once again he stays as close as he can to Mark's wording – retaining the key words 'carpenter', 'son' and 'Mary' (= mother). But he changes their relationship just enough to eliminate the possibly insulting implication. The result is that the second question is slightly more awkward ('Is not his mother called Mary?'), but the basic sense is the same. Once again then we see a concern to hold as closely as possible to the tradition, combined with a willingness to change the sense of the tradition.

The second example of Matthew correcting Mark comes at the beginning of their accounts of the rich young man meeting Jesus.

THE RICH YOUNG MAN

Matt. 19.16–30	Mark 10.17–31	Luke 18.18–30
	¹⁷ And as he was setting out on his journey, a man ran up	
¹⁶ And behold, one came up to him,	and knelt before him, and asked him, 'Good Teacher, what	¹⁸ And a ruler asked him, 'Good Teacher, what
saying, 'Teacher, what good deed must I do, to have eternal life?' ¹⁷ And he said to him, 'Why do you ask me about what is good? One there is who is good. If you would enter life, keep the commandments.' ¹⁸ He said to him, 'Which?' And Jesus said, 'You shall not	must I do to inherit eternal life?' ¹⁸ And Jesus said to him, 'Why do you call me good? No one is good but God alone. ¹⁹ You know the commandments:	shall I do to inherit eternal life?' ¹⁹ And Jesus said to him, 'Why do you call me good? No one is good but God alone. ²⁰ You know the commandments:
kill, You shall not commit adultery, You shall not steal, You shall not bear false witness, ¹⁹ Honor your father and mother, and, You shall love your neighbor as yourself.' ²⁰ The young	'Do not kill, Do not commit adultery, Do not steal, Do not bear false witness, Do not defraud, Honor your father and mother." '	'Do not commit adultery, Do not kill, Do not steal, Do not bear false witness, Do not defraud, Honor your father and mother." '
man said to him, 'All these I have observed; what do I still lack?' ²¹ Jesus said to him, 'If you would be perfect, go, sell what you possess and give to the poor, and you will have treasure in heaven; and come, follow me.'	²⁰ And he said to him, 'Teacher, all these I have observed from my youth.' ²¹ And Jesus looking upon him loved him, and said to him, 'You lack one thing; go, sell what you have, and give to the poor, and you will have treasure in heaven; and come, follow me.'	²¹ And he said 'All these I have observed from my youth.' ²² And when Jesus heard it, he said to him, 'One thing you still lack. Sell all that you have, and distribute to the poor, and you will have treasure in heaven; and come, follow me.'

In this case it would appear that it was the opening exchange between the man and Jesus which caused the problems. The man addresses Jesus as '*Good* teacher'. And Jesus replies with a mild rebuke: 'Why do you call me good? No one is good but God alone' (Mark 10.17–18). Luke sees no difficulty with these words and reproduces them more or less exactly. Not so with Matthew – as we see from the synopsis. The difficulty for Matthew presumably lay in the fact that Jesus was being shown by Mark to disclaim any right to the description 'good'. And by his own logic, Jesus was thereby disclaiming any right to be regarded as divine. If only God is 'good', and Jesus rebukes the address 'Good teacher', the most obvious corollary is that Jesus is not God.

Once again Matthew solves the problem by modifying Mark's wording. And once again the surgery is very neat and delicate. For in this case too he stays as close as he can to Mark's wording and reduces the alteration to a minimum. First he alters the wording of the man's initial question by moving the word 'good' from the address and by putting it as the object of the sentence –

Mark – 'Good teacher, what   must I do . . .'
Matt. – 'Teacher, what   good deed must I do . . .'

That is enough to resolve the potential problem posed by Mark. But, of course, that initial alteration means that Jesus' reply in Mark's version makes less sense. So a second modification is required. Here too Matthew stays as close as he can to Mark's wording. The first sentence of Jesus' reply causes little difficulty, even if Matthew's version seems rather more stilted.

Mark – 'Why do you call me good?'
Matt. – 'Why do you ask me about what is good?'

Jesus' second sentence according to Mark would appear to be less relevant to Matthew's version, since it was responding directly to the Markan address, 'Good teacher'. Matthew indeed might well have omitted it altogether, since it made less sense in his revised version. But evidently in this case too he wanted to stay as close as possible to the traditional wording of the opening dialogue. So he keeps his modification to a minimum and retains the words of Jesus, despite their irrelevance and lack of coherency in his form of the story.

Mark – 'No one is good but God alone';
Matt. – 'One there is who is good'.

When all these factors are taken into consideration, the case for seeing here a revision of Mark's account by Matthew seems to be overwhelming. Whereas it must be judged far less likely that Mark's version was formed as a modification of Matthew. The awkwardness of Matthew's version is *stylistic* and most obviously to be explained as an attempt to deal with the *theological* awkwardness of Mark's version. It is less likely that Mark introduced the theological problem as a way of dealing with the awkwardness of Matthew's style. Least likely of all is it that there are two different incidents recalled here or that the opening exchange in the one incident included both versions!

More important for our present purpose is the confirmation this example provides for the main claim being made in this chapter. On the one hand we see that the central point of the exchange between the man and Jesus is left unaffected. In both cases the man asks what he needs to do to inherit or have eternal life. It is only what we might call the sub-plot (the play on the word 'good') which is affected by Matthew's modification of Mark. Moreover, Matthew's concern to stay as close as possible to Mark's wording is impressive. There is no evidence whatsoever here of a cavalier attitude to the memory of Jesus' words or of a willingness to play fast and loose with the tradition. On the other hand, the fact remains that Matthew *did* alter Mark's wording. Evidently Matthew did feel free to modify the detail of the tradition and did *not* see his task as that of recording word and action with meticulous accuracy. Here again, then, the solid core of *historical information* is clear. But the *interpretative* use of it no less so.

Different versions

A final set of examples shows that traditions stemming from Jesus were used, and so remembered, in *different versions*. We may itemize here some of the best known of the traditions of Jesus' teaching. First, *the Beatitudes*.

THE BEATITUDES

Matt. 5.3–12	Luke 6.20–23

3 'Blessed are the poor in spirit,
    for theirs is the kingdom of heaven.

20 'Blessed are you poor,
    for yours is the kingdom of God.

4 'Blessed are those who mourn,
    for they shall be comforted.
5 'Blessed are the meek,
    for they shall inherit the earth.
6 'Blessed are those who hunger and thirst **for righteousness,**
    for they shall be satisfied.

21 'Blessed are you that hunger now,

    for you shall be satisfied.

7 'Blessed are the merciful,
    for they shall obtain mercy.

'Blessed are you that weep now,
    for you shall laugh.

8 'Blessed are the pure in heart,
    for they shall see God.
9 'Blessed are the peacemakers,
    for they shall be called sons of God.
10 'Blessed are those who are persecuted
    for righteousness' sake,
    for theirs is the kingdom of heaven.
11 'Blessed are you when men revile you and persecute you and utter all kinds of evil against you falsely on my account.
12 Rejoice and be glad, for your reward is great in heaven, for so men persecuted the prophets who were before you.

22 'Blessed are you when men hate you, and when they exclude you and revile you and cast out your name as evil, on account of the Son of man!
23 Rejoice in that day, and leap for joy, for behold, your reward is great in heaven; for so their fathers did to the prophets.'

As the underlining and bold type makes clear, what we have here is two different collections of Jesus' beatitudes.

On the one hand they include the *same* individual beatitudes, even if again in different versions. The first beatitude in each case obviously derives from the same original. Matthew's second beatitude (v. 4) is a variant version of Luke's third (v. 21b) – different wording, but the same basic contrast in view. Matthew's fourth beatitude (v. 6) is clearly a version of Luke's second (v. 21a). And the final beatitude in each case (Matt. verse 11; Luke verse 22) was obviously drawn from the same original template, as also the last sentence ('Rejoice . . .') in each case.

On the other hand, Matthew's version has a further five beatitudes. And if we read on following Luke's account we will see that in the next three verses he has included four 'woes' which exactly match the four 'blessings' (Luke 6.24–26).

The most obvious explanation is that both Matthew and Luke are drawing on what had originally been a single collection of (some of) Jesus' beatitudes. But in the course of transmission, either by the evangelists themselves or by their sources before them, this single collection has been elaborated. A certain amount of interpretation has been included to bring out a particular point (e.g. Matt. 5.6). And other material has been drawn in from elsewhere – different material in each case, so that what in fact developed were two different collections and versions of Jesus' words.

A second example is the even better known *Lord's Prayer*.

THE LORD'S PRAYER

Matt. 6.9–15	Mark 11.25–26	Luke 11.2–4
9 'Pray then like this:		2 And he said to them, 'When you pray, say:
Our <u>Father</u> **who art in heaven,**		'Father,
<u>Hallowed be thy name.</u>		hallowed be thy name.
10 <u>Thy kingdom come,</u>		<u>Thy kingdom come.</u>
Thy will be done		
On earth as it is in heaven.		
11 <u>Give us</u> this <u>day our daily</u> <u>bread;</u>ˢ		3 <u>Give us</u> **each** <u>day our daily</u> <u>bread;</u>ˢ
12 <u>And forgive us our</u> debts,		4 <u>and forgive us our</u> sins,
As <u>we</u> also have <u>forgiven</u> our debtors;		for <u>we</u> ourselves <u>forgive</u> everyone who is <u>indebted</u> to us;
13 <u>And lead us not into temp-</u> <u>tation,</u>		<u>and lead us not into temp-</u> <u>tation.</u>'
But deliver us from evilᵗ.ᵘ		

[14] For if you forgive men
their trespasses, your heavenly
Father also will forgive you;
[15] but if you do not forgive
men their trespasses,[v] neither
will your Father forgive your
trespasses.'

[25] 'And whenever you stand
praying, forgive, if you have
anything against any one; so
that your Father also who is
in heaven may forgive you your
trespasses.'[w]

ˢ Or, our bread for the morrow.   ᵗ Or, the evil one.   ᵘ text: S B D λ it vg bo; **for thine
is the kingdom and the power and the glory, for ever Amen.** W Θ φ K syᵖ sa
Didache.   ᵛ text: B W Θ φ K syᶜ sa bo; omit: their trespasses: S D λ vg syᵖ bo
Augustine.   ʷ text: S B W syˢ sa bo; add verse 26: 'But if you do not forgive, neither will
your Father who is in heaven forgive your trespasses': A C D Θ λ φ K it vg syᵖ Cyprian.

Once again the underlining indicates clearly that we are dealing with
the same prayer. But notice the differences.

On the one hand, Luke's version is significantly briefer. The
opening address of Matthew is longer. And there are two extra
petitions – the third ('Thy will be done . . .'), and the sixth ('But
deliver us from evil'). On the other hand, Luke's has become more
clearly a prayer for regular use – 'Give us *each* day our daily bread'
(v. 3).

The explanation of these differences seems to be straightforward.
In both cases we are probably witnessing the result of liturgical usage.
Hence the longer, more sonorous opening of Matthew – much easier
for a congregation to say together than Luke's abrupt, 'Father'. Hence
too the addition of the third and last petition, which have the effect
of making the whole more balanced, and again more easily recited
in unison. This is just the sort of 'polishing' which we would expect
to find as a result of sustained usage in congregational worship. Luke's
version shows how regular usage shaped the prayer in other congregations of the earliest church.

Furthermore, we should note that the process of liturgical shaping
continued *after* Matthew and Luke had written their Gospels. As we
can see from the line marked out in the footnotes of the text reproduced above, it was only later that the now familiar ending was added
to the Lord's Prayer in Matthew's version – 'For thine is the kingdom
and the power and the glory, for ever. Amen'.

In other words, we can say that Luke's and particularly Matthew's
versions have caught and crystallized the tradition of the Lord's
Prayer at particular points in its earliest liturgical development. The
prayer is indisputably the prayer which Jesus taught his disciples. But
he taught them to *use* it, not simply to remember it as a word taught
them in the past. And in using it their usage shaped it and developed
it into still more usable forms. Clearly there is nothing irresponsible
here. But clearly too the concern of the evangelists goes beyond

the straightforward reproduction and repetition of the precise words taught them by Jesus.

A final example is the equally well known, and in Christian history, even more important tradition of *the words of institution at the Last Supper.*

THE INSTITUTION OF THE LORD'S SUPPER

Matt. 26.26–29	Mark 14.22–25	Luke 22.17–23
See below, v. 29	See below, v. 25	[17] And he took a cup, and when he had given thanks he said, 'Take this, and divide it among yourselves; [18] for I tell you that from now on I shall not drink of the fruit of the vine until the kingdom of God comes.'
[26] Now as they were eating, Jesus took bread, and blessed, and broke it, and gave it to the disciples and said, 'Take, eat; this is my body.'	[22] And as they were eating, he took bread, and blessed, and broke it, and gave it to them and said, 'Take; this is my body.'	[19] And he *took bread, and when he had given thanks he broke it and* gave it to them, saying, *'This is my body* which is given for you. Do this in remembrance of me.'[20] And
[27] And he took a cup, and when he had given thanks he gave it to them, saying, 'Drink of it, all of you; [28] for this is my blood of the[u] covenant, which is poured out for many **for the forgiveness of sins.** [29] I tell you I shall not drink again of this fruit of the vine until that day when I drink it new with you in my Father's kingdom.'*	[23] And he took a cup, and when he had given thanks he gave it to them, and they all drank of it. [24] And he said to them, 'This is my **blood** of the[v] covenant, which is poured out for many. [25] Truly, I say to you, I shall not drink again of the fruit of the vine until that day when I drink it new in the kingdom of God.'*	likewise *the cup after supper,* saying, *'This* **cup** which is poured out for you *is the new covenant in my blood'.*[t] *

* I Corinthians 11.23–25: [23] For I received of the Lord what I also delivered to you, that the Lord Jesus on the night when he was betrayed *took bread,* [24] and when he had given *thanks, he broke it, and* said, '*This is my body which is* broken *for you. Do this in* remembrance of me.' [25] In the same way also *the cup, after supper, saying,* 'This is the *new covenant in my blood.* **Do this, as often as you drink it, in** remembrance of me.'

[t] text: P[75] S A B C W Θ λ φ K it (some MSS) vg sa bo; omit, *which is given for you* through verse 20: D it (some MSS); verses 19, 17, 18: sy[c]; verses 19, 20: sy[p]; verses 19, 20a (*after supper*), 17, 20b (*This blood of mine is the new convenant*): sy[s]. [u] text: P[37] S B Θ; add, *new:* A C D W λ φ K it vg sy[s] sy[p] sa bo. [v] text: S B C D W Θ sa bo; add, *new:* A λ φ K it vg sy[s] sy[p] sa.

Here the matter is rather complex – the complexity probably reflecting the different ways in which these words of Jesus were used in the practice of the Lord's Supper in the earliest churches. I will confine myself to the main features of the text.

What we seem to have here is basically two versions, two different

versions of the words used by Jesus at the Last Supper. One is the
version of Mark, in which he is followed by Matthew; we will call it
M/M. The other is the version common to Luke and Paul – as we
have it in I Cor. 11, and reproduced in the footnote to the text; we
will call it L/P. Both versions are in agreement as to the substance
of what Jesus said, but both the word over the bread and the word
over the cup have rather striking differences.

Consider first the word over the bread:

M/M – 'Take; this is my body';
L/P –   'This is my body which is broken/given for you.
                Do this in remembrance of me.'

It would appear that the common core of Jesus' words ('This is my
body') was remembered or was elaborated in the course of repeated
use in different ways – both quite probably again reflecting liturgical
usage. In the tradition known to Mark the congregation is encouraged
to participate by means of the initial command, 'Take'. In the
tradition used by Paul and Luke the same encouragement comes in
the command to repeat the actions of the Last Supper 'in remembrance of me'. Unlike M/M, the L/P version also has the phrase
'which is broken/given for you'. Either the M/M version did not
consider it necessary to reproduce this explanatory phrase of Jesus,
or, more likely, the phrase has been added as an interpretative expansion to bring out the meaning which was always implicit anyway in
the shorter formula.

With the second word over the cup/wine, the differences are even
great.

M/M – 'This is my blood of the covenant, which is poured out for
        many';
L/P – 'This cup is the new covenant in my blood.'

Individual authors, or the tradition on which they drew, have included
the same sort of interpretative addition or liturgical elaboration:
Matthew – 'for the forgiveness of sins'; Paul – 'Do this, as often as
you drink it, in remembrance of me'. Moreover, Luke also has more
or less the same M/M phrase – 'which is poured out for you'. But
the main difference is that the M/M version focusses on the *blood*,
whereas L/P focusses on the *covenant*. The discussion as to which is
closer to the original word of Jesus is too complex to go into here.
But the sort of argument which weighs with many scholars is the
consideration that 'This is my blood' makes a closer parallel form to
'This is my body', and presumably reflects a stage in the development
of the Lord's Supper when both the bread and the wine had become
a separate action at the end of the meal, with the two words being

said in close conjunction – whereas originally they would have been uttered at different points in the course of a meal (cf. L/P – the cup came 'after supper').

Here again we are pointed to a conclusion which substantiates our original 'Yes and No' answer to the opening question. On the one hand, it is clear that the meaning and substance of the words originally uttered by Jesus have been preserved and faithfully transmitted. Even on the strictest grounds of historical scholarship it must be judged highly likely that Jesus originated the ritual acts of sharing bread and wine as representing his body and blood which Christians practise to this day. On the other hand, it is equally clear that the meaning and substance of Jesus' words were counted more important than any verbal accuracy in transmission. Evidently such differences as we have noted in the three examples above caused no problem for the first Christians. For them the words of Jesus were not the limbs of a dead tradition stiffened and fixed by *rigor mortis*, to be conveyed from place to place like much revered relics, but the voice of a living tradition, which grew as living things do, and spoke with different tone and force to the different situations in which they were recalled and treasured.

Conclusions

So, to conclude, has New Testament scholarship undermined the historical value of the Gospels? We have tried to look at the Gospels as scholars do. That is, to look at the Gospels as they are. To be sure, we have looked at only a few examples. We could have chosen more of the same kind, or other examples to illustrate other features. And much of the material is more complex than the relatively straight-forward cases reviewed above. But hopefully these examples are enough to demonstrate the force of our original answer. Has New Testament scholarship undermined the historical value of the Gospels? Yes and No!

Yes! – but only for the person who comes to the Gospels with expectations they were not designed to fulfil. Whoever looks for chronological accounts, detailed conciseness in every episode recorded, pedantic precision in reproducing Jesus' teaching as given, word for word, and such like, *will* be disappointed. But *not* because of anything scholars have said or done. Rather because the evangelists themselves were not concerned with such matters. The fault here, if fault there be, lies not in the scholars or in their findings, but in the false expectations with which so many have come to the Gospels. The failure, if failure there be, is failure to take the Gospels as they are, on their own terms, the failure to recognize their own emphases and priorities and concerns.

No! – because all these traditions of which we have given examples go back to Jesus and his ministry. All are firmly rooted in the earliest memories of his mission. In conveying the traditions of Jesus' words and deeds the evangelists were concerned to present the tradition in ways that spoke most powerfully to their readers. So while it is ever the first memories of Jesus which they retell, they do so in words often shaped by the circumstances and needs for which they were retold.

In short, far from accusing New Testament scholarship of undermining our common faith, we should be the more grateful to them. For in drawing our attention to the actual features of the Gospels themselves they have helped us the better to understand the purposes and priorities of the Gospel writers and so helped us also to hear their message more clearly.

Note on Professor Wells' View

Professor G. A. Wells, Professor of German in the University of London, has concluded from Paul's virtual silence regarding Jesus' own ministry and teaching that the Jesus of the Gospels never existed. *Jesus: the Evidence* rightly noted that his view is shared by almost no other scholar, but still gave the view some prominence. Suffice it to underline the fact that the relative silence of Paul regarding 'the historical Jesus' is well known to all scholars working in this area. None that I know of shares Professor Wells' opinion. Other explanations are much more plausible. For example, that Paul was so absorbed by his faith in the risen and exalted Christ that he had little need or occasion to refer back to Jesus' earthly ministry apart from the central episode of his death and resurrection. Or, that the traditions about Jesus were sufficiently familiar to his congregations and non-controversial, so that he need do no more than allude to them, as he quite often does.

The alternative thesis that within thirty years there had evolved such a coherent and consistent complex of traditions about a non-existent figure such as we have in the sources of the Gospels is just too implausible. It involves too many complex and speculative hypotheses, in contrast to the much simpler explanation that there was a Jesus who said and did more or less what the first three Gospels attribute to him. The fact of Christianity's beginnings and the character of its earliest tradition is such that we could only deny the existence of Jesus by hypothesizing the existence of some other figure who was a sufficient cause of Christianity's beginnings – another figure who on careful reflection would probably come out very like Jesus!

2 Did Jesus Claim to be the Son of God?

The second major claim made by the programme *Jesus: the Evidence*, which many Christians found disturbing, relates directly to Jesus himself. 'New Testament scholarship has steadily eroded confidence . . . in the image of Jesus as the Son of God.' Or, in the narrower form which makes it possible for us to handle the topic within a single chapter, Has New Testament scholarship shown it to be improbable that Jesus claimed to be the Son of God? The churches could live with some questioning of the historical value of the New Testament. But questions posed about Jesus himself come closer to the nerve centre of the Christian faith. So here too we must ask, Is the claim correct? Is Christian belief in Jesus as Son of God rooted in what we know of Jesus in the Gospels? Or is it rather undermined by what we can know of Jesus' own self-understanding? Did Jesus himself lay claim to that title (Son of God) by which he has been consistently known since then?

Here too, I am afraid, the answer is Yes and No! New Testament scholarship has shown it to be probable that Jesus thought of himself as God's son, or, if you will, God's Son (though it would be unwise to let the discussion turn upon the use or non-use of a capital letter). So, in that sense, Yes! But it has also shown that the full Christian claim (Jesus is *the* Son of God) is almost certainly the product of some development over the first decades of the new movement. So, in that sense, No! Once more, let me explain.

The Jesus of John's Gospel

Did Jesus claim to be the Son of God? At first sight, the answer is a straightforward and unequivocal Yes! In John's Gospel Jesus speaks repeatedly of God as Father and of himself as Son. Indeed, some people express surprise that this question should ever be asked in the first place. The answer is so obvious. And almost always they have the presentation of Jesus in John's Gospel in mind. Consider, for example, the following passage from John 5.16–27:

This was why the Jews persecuted Jesus, because he did this [healed the paralysed man] on the sabbath. But Jesus answered them, 'My Father is working still, and I am working'. This was why the Jews sought all the more to kill him, because he not only broke the sabbath but also called God his own Father, making himself equal with God. Jesus said to them, 'Truly, truly, I say to you, the Son can do nothing of his own accord, but only what he sees the Father doing; for whatever he does, that the Son does likewise. For the Father loves the Son, and shows him all that he himself is doing; and greater works than these will he show him, that you may marvel. For as the Father raises the dead and gives them life, so also the Son gives life to whom he will. The Father judges no one, but has given all judgment to the Son, that all my honour the Son, even as they honour the Father. He who does not honour the Son does not honour the Father who sent him. Truly, truly, I say to you, he who hears my word and believes him who sent me, has eternal life; he does not come into judgment, but has passed from death to life. Truly, truly, I say to you, the hour is coming, and now is, when the dead will hear the voice of the Son of God, and those who hear will live. For as the Father has life in himself, so he has granted the Son also to have life in himself, and has given him authority to execute judgment, because he is the Son of man. . . .

So the answer seems obvious. Of course Jesus claimed to be the Son of God. John's Gospel is clear on the point.

There is, however, a problem here – the question of *whether we can use John's Gospel as direct testimony to Jesus' own teaching*. It is a problem posed not so much by New Testament scholars as by John's Gospel itself. The problem was not *invented* by modern scholarship; it was rather *discovered* by modern scholarship. And since John's Gospel is such a crucial factor in the question asked by this chapter, we must go into it with some care before we can begin to understand why a Yes *and* No answer has to be given.

There is another reason why it is worth pausing at this point to look more closely at John's Gospel. For on the question of the *historical* value of John's Gospel there is probably one of the biggest gulfs between New Testament scholarship and 'the man in the pew'. In preaching and devotional Bible study the assumption is regularly made that all four Gospels are straightforward historical sources for information about what Jesus did or said. Whereas scholars have almost always found themselves pushed to the conclusion that John's Gospel reflects much more of the *early churches'* understanding of Jesus than of Jesus' *own* self-understanding. There is Christian interpretation in the other three Gospels, as we have seen, but in John's Gospel there is much more of it. Again, evangelical or apologetic assertions regarding the claims of Christ will often quote the claims made by Jesus himself (in the Gospel of John) with the alternatives posed, 'Mad, bad or God', without allowing that there may be a further alternative (viz. *Christian* claims about Jesus rather than Jesus' claims about himself). Or again, ecumenical pronouncements will frequently cite Jesus' prayer, 'that they may all be one' (John 17.21), without ever raising the question as to whether the prayer was formulated by Jesus himself or at a later date.

How then are we to understand John's Gospel? The issue here is obviously a peculiarly sensitive one. And the answer to it will have wide repercussions on our use of John's Gospel at all these different levels (preaching, evangelism, etc.). It is important therefore that the Christian community at large should recognize *how* scholars see John's Gospel and *why* they see it that way. That is our task here. Once again it is too big a task for a single chapter, so the presentation has to be illustrative rather than comprehensive.

The Problem of John's Gospel

How are we to understand the Gospel of John? Is it a source of historical information about Jesus' teaching and self-understanding? The issue arises because John's Gospel is so obviously *different from the other three Gospels* – particularly in its representation of Jesus' teaching. The point can be illustrated in a simple table.

Jesus' teaching	Synoptic Gospels	John's Gospel
Style	epigrams, parables	long, often involved discourses
Content	kingdom of God hardly anything about himself	Jesus himself (I ams) hardly anything about the kingdom

Jesus' teaching style

For examples of Jesus' teaching style in the *Synoptics* we need only think of the sort of material grouped by Matthew in the Sermon on the Mount.

> You are the salt of the earth; but if salt has lost its taste, how shall its saltness by restored? It is no longer good for anything except to be thrown out and trodden under foot by men.
> You are the light of the world. A city set on a hill cannot be hid. Nor do men light a lamp and put it under a bushel, but on a stand, and it gives light to all in the house. Let your light so shine before men, that they may see your good works and give glory to your Father who is in heaven (Matt. 5.13–16).

Do not lay up for yourselves treasures on earth, where moth and rust consume and where thieves break in and steal, but lay up for yourselves treasure in heaven, where neither moth nor rust consumes and where thieves do not break in and steal. For where your treasure is, there will your heart be also.

The eye is the lamp of the body. So, if your eye is sound, your whole body will be full of light; but if your eye is not sound, your whole body will be full of darkness. If then the light in you is darkness, how great is the darkness!

No one can serve two masters; for either he will hate the one and love the other, or he will be devoted to the one and despise the other. You cannot serve God and mammon (Matt. 6.19–24).

For Jesus' *epigrammatic* style we may consider, for example, the collection of proverbial sayings which we find in Mark 4, and which must have been quite popular since they appear elsewhere in different contexts.

Is a lamp brought in to be put under a bushel, or under a bed, and not on a stand? (Mark 4.21 = Matt. 5.15 = Luke 8.16 = Luke 11.33 = Gospel of Thomas 33).

For there is nothing hid, except to be made manifest; nor is anything secret, except to come to light (Mark 4.22 = Matt. 10.26 = Luke 8.17 = Luke 12.2 = Gospel of Thomas 5 and 6).

If any man has ears to hear, let him hear (Mark 4.23 = Mark 4.9 = Mark 7.16(?) = Gospel of Thomas 8, 21, 63, 65 and 96).

Take heed what you hear; the measure you give will be the measure you get, and still more will be given you (Mark 4.24 = Luke 8.18 and 6.38 = Matt. 7.2).

For to him who has will more be given; and from him who has not, even what he has will be taken away (Mark 4.25 = Matt. 13.12 = Luke 8.18 = Luke 19.26 = Gospel of Thomas 41).

For *parables* we need only refer to such justly famous stories as the Good Samaritan, the Prodigal Son, the Sower and his Seed, the Two Debtors, and so on (Luke 10.29–35; Luke 15.11–32; Mark 4.3–8; Matt. 18.23–34), well known to generations of Sunday School and day school children. All of them are characterized by the skill of a brilliant story teller. They sketch a vivid picture in a few words; they utilize the homely and familiar with powerful effect; there is in each in greater or less degree a dramatic surge which carries the listener forward, even in mini-parables like the Treasure in the Field and the Pearl of Great Price (Matt. 13.44–46). Jesus understood well the fascination which people find in the dramas and unexpected turns of everyday life.

Contrast the teaching style of *John's* Gospel.

Jesus answered them, 'Do not murmur among yourselves. No one can come to me unless the Father who sent me draws him; and I will raise him up at the last day. It is written in the prophets, "And they shall all be taught by God". Everyone who has heard and learned from the Father comes to me. Not that any one has seen the Father except him who is from God; he has seen the Father. Truly, truly, I say to you, he who believes has eternal life. I am the bread of life. Your fathers ate the manna in the wilderness, and they died. This is the bread which comes down from heaven, that a man may eat of it and not die. I am the living bread which came down from heaven; if any one eats of this bread, he will live for ever; and the bread which I shall give for the life of the world is my flesh (John 6.43–51).

I am the true vine, and my Father is the vinedresser. Every branch of mine that bears no fruit, he takes away, and every branch that does bear fruit he prunes, that it may bear more fruit. You are already made clean by the word which I have spoken to you. Abide in me, and I in you. As the branch cannot bear fruit by itself, unless it abides in the vine, neither can you, unless you abide in me. I am the vine, you are the branches. He who abides in me, and I in him, he it is that bears much fruit, for apart from me you can do nothing. If a man does not abide in me, he is cast forth as a branch and withers; and the branches are gathered, thrown into the fire and burned. If you abide in me, and my words abide in you, ask whatever you will, and it shall be done for you. By this my Father is glorified, that you bear much fruit, and so prove to be my disciples. As the Father has loved me, so have I loved you; abide in my love. If you keep my commandments, you will abide in my love, just as I have kept my Father's commandments and abide in his love. These things I have spoken to you, that my joy may be in you, and that your joy may be full (John 15.1–11).

Clearly, this is a different world from the Synoptics. The ideas and their elaboration are much more abstruse. There is a similarity in the homely imagery used – bread, vine – but the way that imagery is used is quite markedly removed from the epigrams and parables which characterize the Synoptics.

The content of Jesus' teaching

As to the difference in content between the Synoptics and John, it is almost sufficient to present the statistical facts for the number of times the word 'kingdom' appears on Jesus' lips and the number of times he uses 'I' in self-reference.

	Matthew	Mark	Luke	John
Kingdom	47	18	37	5
I	17	9	10	118

When we read the Synoptic Gospels the impression is strong that 'kingdom' was a key word in Jesus' preaching and teaching, particularly 'the kingdom of God'. For example, Mark deliberately begins his account of Jesus' proclamation with what he evidently intended as a summary statement characterizing Jesus' ministry as a whole – 'After John was arrested, Jesus came into Galilee, preaching the gospel of God, and saying, "The time is fulfilled, and the kingdom of God is at hand . . ." ' (Mark 1.14–15). According to Matthew and Luke, when Jesus extended his mission by sending out his disciples in turn, it is the same message which he gave them – 'The kingdom of God is at hand' (Matt. 10.7; Luke 10.9). And the largest single group of parables are those which begin, 'The kingdom of God/ heaven is like . . .'.

Contrast John's Gospel, where Jesus is *never* shown as preaching or proclaiming the kingdom; and the five occurrences of the phrase are confined to *two* passages – in the conversations with Nicodemus (John 3.3, 5) and with Pilate (John 18.36). And in the latter case the talk is exceptionally of '*my* kingdom' rather than 'the kingdom of God'.

The contrast between the Synoptics and John seems to be less striking in the case of the 'I'-statements. But in fact almost all the Synoptic references are of a conventional kind, even where the 'I' is emphatic. Whereas the Johannine usage is full of profound and often staggering claims. Particularly the seven well known 'I am' sayings: 'I am the bread of life' (6.35); 'I am the light of the world' (8.12); 'I am the door of the sheep' (10.7); 'I am the good shepherd' (10.11); 'I am the resurrection and the life' (11.25); 'I am the way, and the truth and the life' (14.6); 'I am the true vine' (15.1); and the most striking 'I am' saying of all – 'Before Abraham was, I am' (8.58).

The contrast between the Synoptics and John at both these points is therefore not merely statistical. There is a qualitative contrast too. This again is not something imposed upon or read in by New Testament scholars. The contrast is there, in the Gospels themselves. New Testament scholarship simply tries to explain what is *there*. The contrast is not to be exaggerated or overdramatized. But it is there. How is it to be explained?

Explanations for the Differences between the Synoptics and John

There are, broadly speaking, *three* possible explanations for the rather striking contrasts between the Synoptic Gospels and John's Gospel.

Wholly historical

One explanation attempts to argue for a high degree of historicity. On this view, it is not necessary to sacrifice belief in the historical value of John's Gospel in order to maintain the historical value of the Synoptics. They are *all* trustworthy witnesses of what Jesus actually said and did. The reason for the differences between them in style and content is simply that Jesus used different styles and different material for different audiences. In particular, John's Gospel gives us the typical style and content of Jesus' *private* teaching to his disciples, or, an alternative view, the style and content of his controversies with the *Jerusalem* authorities. So the argument would run.

The difficulty with this suggestion is twofold. (*a*) The fact is that it simply does not work. The style of Jesus' teaching is constant *throughout* John's Gospel. It is the same for *all* audiences. Whether it is to the Jewish leader (Nicodemus) in Jerusalem (ch. 3), or to the women in Samaria (4), or to the crowd in Galilee (6), or to the Jerusalem authorities (8), or to the disciples (14–16), or indeed to God in prayer (17), the style is the same. And as it is consistent throughout John, so it is *consistently different* from the Synoptics. The difference is not between geographical settings, public and private, preaching and teaching. The difference is between the Gospels themselves. This suggested explanation fails to provide an explanation.

(*b*) As for content, what are we to make of the fact that this very powerful self-testimony of Jesus runs throughout John's Gospel and yet lacks any real parallel in the Synoptics? In particular, what about these profound 'I am' claims? If they were part of the original words of Jesus himself, how could it be that *only* John has picked them up, and *none* of the others? Call it scholarly scepticism if you will, but I must confess that I find it almost incredible that such sayings should have been neglected *had* they been known as a feature of Jesus' teaching. If the 'I ams' *had* been part of the original tradition, it is very hard indeed to explain why none of the other three evangelists made use of them. Most scholars therefore find themselves forced by the evidence to look for another explanation.

Wholly theological

At the opposite end of the spectrum of possible explanations is the view that John's Gospel has *no historical value at all*. An understandable reaction against the unreality of the first explanation is to argue that John's Gospel is the complete creation of John the evangelist himself, from start to finish – theological, or spiritual in character, and *not* historical. This line of argument was quite popular among many scholars a hundred years ago. But it is a good deal less popular today.

(*a*) It would now be widely acknowledged that John's Gospel is valuable as a historical source, at least to the extent that it preserves good historical tradition – in some cases known to the Synoptics, in other cases not known or not used by the Synoptics. For example, John provides some very important information about the very earliest days of Jesus' ministry. The Synoptic Gospels *begin* their account of Jesus' ministry *after* the Baptist has been removed from the scene (Matt. 4.12; Mark 1.14). But the abruptness with which Jesus summons his first disciples (Matt. 4.18–22; Mark 1.16–20) has always been something of a puzzle. John's Gospel helps to fill out the picture. For John's Gospel shows that Jesus' earliest period of ministry overlapped with that of the Baptist (John 3.22–23) and that there were earlier encounters between Jesus and his first disciples during that period (John 1.35–42).

As another example we may simply refer to the various geographical notes which are scattered within the Gospel of John, thirteen of them not mentioned in the Synoptics. Such references as to 'Aenon near Salim' (John 3.23) or to the pool of Siloam (9.7), indicate a pretty fair and confident knowledge, which, when we can check it, proves to be accurate. The best example of this is the reference to the pool in Jerusalem with five porticoes, the pool of Bethzatha or Bethesda (5.2). For centuries the site of this pool had been forgotten, and the question posed as to whether the odd number of *five* colonnades was symbolical rather than historical. But in a series of excavations from 1914 to 1938 the pool itself was rediscovered within Jerusalem, and the discovery confirmed that there must indeed have been five porticoes, since it was in fact a double pool, or two pools, with the fifth colonnade running between them. With such historical accuracy of geographical detail, it is hardly plausible to argue that the whole Gospel is the creation of the evangelist's imagination. At the very least his material must be firmly rooted in good historical tradition, that is, in the testimony or account of eyewitnesses.

(*b*) It is of course with the *teaching* of Jesus within John's Gospel that the issue we are now discussing comes to its sharpest focus. Here too it has become steadily clearer during the last few decades that these long and involved discourses cannot be treated simply as creations of the evangelist. Again and again it can be shown with a high degree of probability that they are dependent in some measure at least on traditions which go back to Jesus. In fact, many of the

discourses in John's Gospel seem to grow out of elements of Jesus'
teaching as recorded in the other three Gospels.

A good example of this is Jesus' teaching on the new birth to
Nicodemus in John 3.1–15. The central challenge posed by Jesus is
closely paralleled by a saying which appears in slightly different
versions in Matt. 18.3, Mark 10.15 and Luke 18.17.

John   – Truly, truly, I say to you, unless one is born anew,
                      he cannot see the kingdom of God.
Matt.   – Truly,   I say to you, unless you turn and become
               like children you will never enter the kingdom of
               heaven.
Mark/Luke – Truly,   I say to you, whoever does not receive
               the kingdom of God like a child shall not enter it.

What is particularly interesting here is that this is the only passage in
John where Jesus speaks of the kingdom of God in language
approaching that of the Synoptics. John 3 seems to be an elaboration
of that basic claim made by Jesus.

Another example is John 6.51–58, which seems to be a variation
or reflection on the words of the Last Supper: 'This is my body (which
is given for you) . . . This is my blood of the covenant poured out
for many . . .' (Mark 14.22–24; Luke 22.19–20). In John 6 Jesus says:

> . . . the bread which I shall give for the life of the world is my flesh . . .
> Unless you eat the flesh of the Son of man and drink his blood, you
> have no life in you; he who eats my flesh and drinks my blood has
> eternal life, and I will raise him up at the last day. For my flesh is food
> indeed, and my blood is drink indeed . . .

For a final example we may turn to John 10. The presentation of
Jesus as the good shepherd who lays down his life for the sheep and
who has other sheep which he must bring into the fold makes a
powerful impression (John 10, particularly verses 11 and 16). The
basic theme is close to that of the parable of the lost sheep (Luke
15.4–6), and John 10 looks very much like a developed variation of
that parable. In this case the development consists in the wholly
natural identification of Jesus himself with the shepherd of Jesus'
parable. John 10, in other words, can be most simply understood as
a Christian retelling of Jesus' own parable in the light of Jesus' death
and resurrection.

In short, the second alternative explanation of the differences
between the Synoptics and John will not work either. To argue that
John's presentation of Jesus' ministry and teaching is wholly the
product of John's creative imagination, purely theological and not at

all historical, is to fly in the face of the evidence. There are too many indications that John's portrayal is in touch with or draws upon good historical information about what Jesus did and said.

Theological elaboration of history

The third position comes somewhere in the middle between the other two. It tries to take account of the evidence which tells against both of the more extreme positions. With reference to Jesus' teaching, where the issue is at its sharpest for us, it concludes that the discourses of Jesus are neither straightforward history nor straight theology, but a combination of both history and theology. The best explanation of these two sets of different features is that *the discourses are meditations or indeed sermons on typical episodes in Jesus' ministry and on particular teachings of Jesus.* The sort of considerations which have pushed scholars in this direction can be easily documented.

(*a*) The discourses of John's Gospel are often constructed round themes and grow out of particular episodes. This is simply an elaboration of the point made above (p. 38). In some cases there is more than one theme, and the use of the dialogue form sometimes makes the development of the theme(s) less clear to a first reading now. The most obvious examples of a single theme discourse are in John 4 (on the water of life – vv.7–15) and John 6 (on the bread of life – vv.25–58). For examples of the way in which the discourse or theme grows out of particular incidents we may consider chapter 5 (on Jesus' proper work, growing out of the healing on the sabbath) and chapter 9 (on true sight and blindness). The bread of life discourse obviously grows out of the feeding of the 5,000 (John 6).

John 6.25–58 indeed is one of the best examples we possess of a Jewish sermon (or midrash) for that period. To print it all would require too much space, but it is well worth pausing at this point to read it in a modern translation (vv.43–51 are reproduced above on p. 34). Anyone who does read it as a whole will notice how the discourse is constructed round a basic contrast (not material bread, but the true bread), in which the second half of the contrast is elaborated and developed in what seems like a circular motion, where the argument keeps returning to the same point and restating it afresh. This elaboration itself has two interacting themes. The main theme identifies the one who gives the true bread as the Father (not Moses), and the true bread as Jesus himself. It is the latter strand on which much of the development concentrates as the full implications of what Jesus is saying are brought home. The counterpoint is formed by the corollary theme of eating the bread: eating the one kind of bread resulted in death; eating the other results in life.

The complete theme is first announced in v.27: 'Do not labour for the food which perishes, but for the food which endures to eternal life.' This allusion to food which perishes is elaborated by reference to the manna of the wilderness period (v.31) which the fathers ate and died (vv.49,58). The key text on which the positive side of the contrast is developed is v.31: 'He gave them bread from heaven to eat' (a combination of Exodus 16.4, 15 and Ps. 78.24). This in fact is the text for the sermon and it is the exposition of this text which forms the main thrust of the sermon. He who gives the bread is God, the Father (vv.32,44,58). The bread which is given is Jesus himself, the true bread (v.32), the bread of life (vv.35,48) which has come down from heaven (vv.41,51), the bread given for the life of the world (v.51), Jesus' flesh (vv.51,53–56). To eat this bread (that is, to believe in this Jesus) is the means to eternal life (vv.35,47,50–51, 54,57–58). Verse 58 provides the fitting conclusion in which the central themes are rounded off in an appropriate summary: 'This is the bread which came down from heaven, not such as the fathers ate and died; he who eats this bread will live for ever' (6.58).

The whole passage gives the very strong impression of a very skilfully constructed sermon. Indeed, it is not difficult to visualize one of the early church groups with whom the evangelist worshipped listening in rapt attention to just such an exposition of the significance of Jesus, their Lord and Saviour, as they prepared to share together the bread and wine, his flesh and blood.

(b) The style of John's Gospel is also the style of the letters of John. Compare, for example, John 8.34–36, 44–47 with I John 3.4–10.

John 8 – Jesus answered them, 'Truly, truly, I say to you, everyone who commits sin is a slave to sin. The slave does not continue in the house for ever; the son continues for ever. So if the Son makes you free, you will be free indeed . . .'. '. . . You are of your father the devil, and your will is to do your father's desires. He was a murderer from the beginning, and has nothing to do with the truth, because there is no truth in him. When he lies, he speaks according to his own nature, for he is a liar and the father of lies. But, because I tell the truth, you do not believe me. Which of you convicts me of sin? If I tell the truth, why do you not believe me? He who is of God hears the words of God; the reason why you do not hear them is that you are not of God.'

I John 3 – Everyone who commits sin is guilty of lawlessness; sin is lawlessness. You know that he appeared to take away sins, and in him there is no sin. No one who abides in him sins; no one who sins has either seen him or known him. Little children, let no one deceive you. He who does right is righteous, as he is righteous. He who commits sin is of the devil; for the devil has sinned from the beginning. The reason the Son of God appeared was to destroy the works of the devil. No one born of God commits sin; for God's nature abides in him, and he cannot sin because he is born of God. By this it may be seen who are the children of God, and who are the children of the devil: whoever does not do right is not of God, nor he who does not love his brother.

The style of these two passages is clearly very much of a piece. The teaching of *John* in John's *Epistle* is the same as the teaching of *Jesus* in John's *Gospel*, apart, of course, from the considerable amount of self-testimony in the latter. The style, in other words, is the style of *John*. However much the content goes back to Jesus, it has been passed through the medium of John's thought and language.

By way of confirmation we need simply note that the same is true of the teaching of *John the Baptist* in John's Gospel. The character of much of the Baptist's message in the Fourth Gospel is far closer to that of the Gospel and of the Johannine Epistles than to the character of his preaching as recorded in the other three Gospels (cf. John 3.27–30 with 3.31–36 and contrast it with Matt. 3.7–10). Where John the Baptist and Jesus speak with such a different voice from that recorded in the Synoptics and with the same voice which we find to be typical of the writer(s) of John's Gospel and Epistles, it is hard to avoid the conclusion that it is the *same* voice which we are hearing each time – the voice of John.

(*c*) One other strand of evidence leads most scholars to the conclusion that John's Gospel was not written until the last ten or fifteen years of the first century AD. And also that the content of the Gospel itself reflects something of these later circumstances in which it was written. To be more precise, the discourses of the Fourth Gospel reflect a breach between the followers of Jesus and 'the Jews' which did not take place till the 80s.

The evidence here is twofold. In the first place, there is the very striking use of the phrase 'the Jews'. In John's Gospel it occurs about seventy times, in contrast to the five or six occurrences in the Synoptics. That would be somewhat surprising in itself. But what is even more noticeable is that the phrase has become more or less a stereotype for Jesus' opponents, a technical term for the religious authorities in their hostility to Jesus. What is most remarkable is the way in which individuals, who are themselves Jews, are nevertheless distinguished from 'the Jews'. In 5.15 we read, 'The man went away and told the Jews that it was Jesus who had healed him'. A Jew told 'the Jews'! Similarly in 7.13: 'for fear of the Jews no one spoke openly of him'. Jews fear 'the Jews'! Similarly in 9.22: the parents of the man who had been blind 'said this because they feared the Jews'. Here again, Jews fear 'the Jews'!

This last reference leads us into the second strand of evidence. For in 9.22 the evangelist continues –

> . . . for the Jews had already agreed that if anyone should confess him (Jesus) to be the Christ, he was to be put out of the synagogue.

Here we read of an official decision reached by the Jewish authorities in Jerusalem ('the Jews') to excommunicate any member of the Jewish community who confessed Jesus as the Messiah. In other words, what is referred to here is the complete breach between official Judaism and Christianity. And this we know did not take place in Palestine till after the destruction of Jerusalem in the 70s. Prior to that time Jews who were believers in Jesus as the Messiah (Christ) were able to continue living as Jews and attending the synagogue. There had of course been tensions, but not over the claim that Jesus was the Messiah. The incident over Stephen seems to have focussed chiefly on his views regarding the temple (Acts 6–7). And the subsequent persecution was primarily motivated by zeal for the law and hostility to Christian unconcern over circumcision and food laws (e.g. Acts 15.1–2; Phil. 3.5–6). But within Judaism there was nothing intrinsically unacceptable or 'heretical' about hailing a particular individual as 'Messiah'. And we have no real evidence of the Christian claim for Jesus at this point becoming unacceptable during the first fifty years of Christianity. Whereas we do have fairly clear indications in Jewish sources that a formal decision was taken by the surviving Jewish authorities in Palestine in the 80s to treat the Nazarenes (that is, those who confessed Jesus of Nazareth as Messiah) as heretics. In other words, John 9.22 seems to reflect that very breach between Judaism and Christianity, that testing time for Jewish Christians when, for the first time, they had to make a final choice between synagogue and the congregation of Jesus' followers, between being a Jew (as now more precisely defined) and being a Christian (cf. 12.42; 16.2).

The point is that this conflict between Jesus and 'the Jews' is part of the warp and woof of so much of the Gospel (particularly the central section, chapters 5–11). It forms an integral part of the structure of several of the discourses and dialogues. This strongly suggests that these discourses have been formulated with that conflict in view, that is, in the light of the growing tension between Jewish authority and Jewish Christian which marked the last two decades of the first century. This section of John's Gospel in particular seems in fact to operate or combine two different levels – the historical level of Jesus' own ministry, when he healed the lame and the blind, and the historical level of the Johannine congregation(s), when many of them must have faced the agonizing choice which is so movingly portrayed as confronting the formerly blind man and his parents in chapter 9. To help his readers make that choice (between synagogue and church, between being a Jew and being Christian), and to strengthen the faith of those who had decided for Jesus the Christ against 'the Jews' was probably one of John's main reasons for writing the Gospel (cf. 20.31).

In the light of all this evidence, most scholars opt for some version of the third alternative (theological elaboration of history). John's Gospel is an account of Jesus refracted through the prism of John's theology and literary style. And the discourses in particular are best seen as meditations or sermons intended to draw out the significance of what Jesus did and said.

The fact that the evangelist presents the discourses as actual dialogues between Jesus and his audiences should not be counted as evidence against this conclusion. John was simply doing what generations of preachers have done since – expanding and developing particular points regarding Jesus through the literary style of the dialogue-discourse. Almost certainly he was not concerned with the sort of questions which trouble some Christians today – Did Jesus actually say this? Did he use these precise words? and so on. It was enough that these words were proper expressions of what was true about Jesus, of what Jesus would have said for himself, for example, to the Jewish believers under threat from the Jewish authorities. Just so might a preacher today retell an episode from Jesus' life (for example, the healing of blind Bartimaeus in Mark 10.46–52), and in the retelling use some historical licence to construct or elaborate various conversations within the crowd, or with Jesus. And just so would it be improper to accuse the preacher of falsehood by ignoring the literary vehicle he was obviously using?

In short, the Jesus of John is not to be identified in a complete way with the Jesus who meets us in the Synoptics. The Jesus of John is *also* Jesus as he was increasingly seen to be, as the understanding of who Jesus was deepened through the decades of the first century. John's Gospel, we may say, is intended to present the *truth* about Jesus, but not by means of a strictly historical portrayal. The Synoptic Gospels, if you like, are more like a portrait of Jesus; John's Gospel is more like an impressionist painting of Jesus. Both present the real Jesus, but in very different ways.

Jesus as the Son of God in John's Gospel

What does all this say about Jesus' teaching in the Fourth Gospel regarding his divine sonship? The long digression just completed was made necessary by the fact that John's Gospel seems to provide the

complete answer to our opening question. Did Jesus claim to be the
Son of God? – John's Gospel seemed to require an unequivocal Yes.
But if now we have had to conclude that John's Gospel was not
intended to provide a strictly historical portrayal, what does that say
about John's presentation of Jesus as the Son of God? Is Jesus' own
testimony as given by John part of the historical core which John has
elaborated, or part of the elaboration? Does Jesus' talk of himself as
'the Son' derive from the earliest traditions of Jesus or from the
subsequent theological reflection on the significance of Jesus?

The initial answer has to be that the self-testimony of Jesus in
John's Gospel belongs in large part at least to the enlarged and
developed picture which John paints. The point can again be
represented statistically, where the key statistic is the number of times
Jesus speaks of God as his Father

	Mark	Q	Luke	Matthew	John
'Father'	3	4	4	31	100
'the Father'	1	1	2	1	73

('Q' is the symbol used to denote what was probably a second source
used by Matthew and Luke – Mark's Gospel itself being the 'first'
source; 'Luke' and 'Matthew' denote the material peculiar to each.)
Since Mark and Q are generally regarded as the earliest of these five,
and John the latest, the most obvious deduction to be drawn from
these statistics is this: over the period spanned by Mark and John
there was a development and expansion of the tradition at this point.
The earliest churches remembered only a few occasions or utterances
in which Jesus spoke of God as his father. But in the last decades of
the first century there seems to have been a tendency to represent
this form of speech as more typical of Jesus. (In Matthew the expansion often comes through the introduction of the typically Matthean
phrase, 'my Father who is in heaven'.) And in John's Gospel this
representation of Jesus has become a central strand for the Gospel
itself.

In other words, we cannot in fairness take John's reported testimony on this point as firm evidence of what Jesus actually said about
himself. On the evidence as we have it, it would be more accurate
to regard the claims of Jesus in John as an integral part of the
exposition of what John and his fellow Christians *had found Jesus to
be*. Such utterances as 'I am the light of the world' (John 8.12) and
'I and the Father are one' (John 10.30) bear testimony to John's
experience of Jesus (during his life *and* since), Jesus' witness to
himself through the Spirit, as John would no doubt want to claim

(John 15.26; 16.12–15), rather than Jesus' witness to himself while on earth – the truth of Jesus in *retro*spect rather than as expressed by Jesus at the time.

But that is not the complete answer. For the *same* evidence shows that this teaching was *not* invented by John. It is rather an enlargement of an element which was *already* present in Jesus' teaching *from the beginning*. It was important for John that the Spirit was revealing to them 'many things' Jesus had not said to them while on earth, many things which glorified Jesus (John 16.12,14). But it was also important for John that the task of the Spirit was to remind them of what Jesus had said while he was still with them (14.25–26). It is likely then that the expanded teaching of Jesus about his divine sonship is just that, expanded teaching of Jesus. Or to put it more precisely, it is likely that this element of Jesus' discourses too has firm roots in the earliest memory of what Jesus had said while with his first disciples. As in other cases the discourses seem to have grown round particular sayings of Jesus which we know of also from the Synoptics (p. 38), so here Jesus' teaching on his divine sonship in John has probably grown round the memory of things Jesus actually did say on the subject. This deduction from within John's Gospel itself is confirmed by a closer study of related testimony in the Synoptics.

Jesus as God's Son in the Synoptic Gospels

The claim that Jesus regarded himself as Son of God is not based only on the testimony of John's Gospel. It is also testified in the traditions used by Matthew, Mark and Luke. In this case too we can see something at least of the historical information on which John's meditations and elaborations are based.

Jesus' own prayer

Particularly worthy of note is the testimony that Jesus addressed God as 'Father' in his praying. There are several important features here. First, it is independently attested in *all* five strands of the Gospel tradition – Mark, Q (the second source of Matthew and Luke), the material peculiar to Luke, the material peculiar to Matthew, and John.

> Mark 14.36 – Jesus' prayer in Gethsemane: 'Abba, Father, all things are possible to thee; remove this cup from me; yet not what I will, but what thou wilt'.
> Q = Matt. 11.25–26 = Luke 10.21 – 'I thank thee, Father, Lord of heaven and earth, that thou hast hidden these things from the

wise and understanding and revealed them to babes; yea, Father,
for such was thy gracious will'.

Luke 23.46 – Jesus' prayer on the cross: 'Father, into thy hands I
commend my spirit'.

Matt. 26.42 – Jesus' second prayer in Gethsemane: 'My Father, if
this cannot pass unless I drink it, thy will be done'.

John 11.41 – Jesus at the tomb of Lazarus: 'Father, I thank thee
that thou hast heard me'.

Second, the testimony is that Jesus almost *always* prayed in this
way. The only time it is clearly attested that Jesus did not address
God as 'Father' was in the experience of desolation on the cross,
when it was the opening of Ps. 22 which came to his lips – 'My God,
my God, why hast thou forsaken me?' For the rest 'Father' was
evidently his usual form of address. Moreover, it was this way of
speaking to God which Jesus evidently encouraged in his disciples,
as Luke's version of the Lord's Prayer shows (Luke 11.2). On this
basis we can say with some confidence that it was customary for Jesus
to approach God as Father, and that this way of addressing God was
wholly characteristic of Jesus and of the manner of praying he both
practised and taught his disciples.

Third, we can use the slightness of the Synoptic testimony also in
favour of this conclusion. For it is clear from the paucity of the
testimony in the Gospels that the evangelists have not made much of
this tradition of Jesus praying to God as Father. This is true even of
the fourth evangelist, despite his considerable elaboration of the
Father/Son language apart from prayer (the one exception is John
17). Where evangelists have not developed a particular theme, it is
normally a good indication of its historicity. As we have now seen,
the Gospel writers show a fair degree of liberty in their choice of
material (what they leave out as well as put in) and in the way they
interpret and use it. So when we find a tradition which they have *not*
built up into a more sustained theme, we can be fairly confident that
that tradition contains a piece of historical information. They have
included it not so much to make a point of *their* choosing, but simply
because it belonged to the memory of Jesus' time on earth.

All these considerations build up for the majority of scholars to
the clear and firm conclusion that as a matter of historical fact Jesus
did address God as 'Father' in his prayer and that this was characteristic of his prayer.

Can we say more? The answer probably is Yes, and it turns on the
word which Jesus used for 'Father' in his prayer.

God as abba

The word Jesus almost certainly used was 'Abba'. This is an Aramaic form for the style of address used by Jesus – 'Father'. It has actually been retained in Mark's version of the prayer in Gethsemane; that is to say, the Aramaic word has been copied into Greek letters, and not merely translated (Mark 14.36).

More striking still is the testimony of Paul in two of his letters that the same form of prayer was regarded as the voice of the Spirit speaking in prayer through the Christian. 'When we cry, "Abba! Father!" it is the Spirit himself bearing witness with our spirit that we are children of God' (Rom. 8.15–16). 'God has sent the Spirit of his Son into our hearts, crying, "Abba! Father!" ' (Gal. 4.6). Why, we may properly ask, should the first Christians retain this Aramaic word rather than be content simply with its Greek equivalent? The answer must be that the Aramaic expression itself had become very well established in Christian prayer from the beginning and was especially treasured by them. And if we ask Why? again, the most obvious answer to come back is that they treasured it so much *because it was so characteristic of Jesus' own prayer*. This in fact is clearly implied in the two passages where Paul speaks of it. For in each case the Spirit's crying 'Abba! Father!' is a clear sign for the Christians that *they* are sons of God and *heirs with Christ* (Rom. 8.16–17; Gal. 4.7). They share in Jesus' sonship and can be confident that this is so because they share in Jesus' prayer!

We can make one further deduction from this evidence. The fact that 'abba' is remembered as particularly characteristic of Jesus' prayer probably implies that it was an *unusual* style of prayer. Had it been the typical style of addressing God in the prayers of the ordinary people of Galilee or of a particular Jewish sect, it would not have been regarded as evidence of the Christian claim to the Spirit and to divine sonship. But since (so far as we can tell) the claim to a share in divine sonship through the Spirit *is* something which marked out the first Christians within the Judaism of the time, the evidence which these Christians cite as proof of that claim must itself have been distinctive. Had 'abba' been widely used outside Christian circles, its use within Christian circles would have proved nothing. It is cited in Romans 8 and Galatians 4, then, precisely because it was remembered as something distinctive – a distinctive bond between Jesus and his disciples, and so distinctive also in its original use by Jesus himself.

Why was it so distinctive of Jesus' own prayer? The most probable answer is that 'Abba' was a *surprising* word to use in addressing God. In its natural usage it was a *family* word and usually confined to the family circle. It was the word with which children would address the head of the family, and so carried with it a considerable note of warm trust as well as of respect. It was a word resonant with family intimacy, probably used by children from earliest years of speech; as we can tell from its very form, it would be one of the earliest words an infant would be able to say. There is no precise equivalent in English, though the older style 'Papa' probably comes closest. The nearest today would be the colloquial 'Dad'.

The point is that to address God in such a colloquial way, with such intimacy, is hardly known in the Judaism of Jesus' time. The regular Jewish prayers were a good deal more dignified, more in the style of the second address used in Matt. 11.25 – Luke 10.21: 'Lord of heaven and earth'. Interestingly enough, the same is true of the typical Muslim today: he will address Allah as the 'All merciful'; but 'Father' is too bold and improper. So too at the time of Jesus. Had most Jews of Jesus' time considered using 'Abba' in addressing God they would probably have rejected it as too intimate, as a mark of irreverence.

Jesus would not have been unaware of this. And yet 'Abba' was his characteristic way of addressing God. Presumably for the same reason: what others thought too intimate in praying to God, Jesus used *because* of its intimacy. The most obvious explanation for Jesus' adoption of just this word as the hallmark of his prayer was that it expressed an intimacy with God which he experienced and relied upon in his relationship with God. He thought of himself before God as a son before his father. Since the 'Abba' prayer is both so characteristic *and* so distinctive of Jesus, it must mean that Jesus naturally or instinctively saw himself as God's son, sustained by that intimate relation with God which only a son close to his father can know.

At this point the discussion could broaden out to consider other key texts in the Synoptics – particularly Matt. 11.27/(Luke 10.22):

All things have been delivered to me by my Father;
and no one knows the Son except the Father
and no one knows the Father except the Son
and anyone to whom the Son chooses to reveal him.

The difficulty here is that scholars cannot agree on this verse, on whether it is a straightforward transcription of Jesus' actual words, or an example of the kind of elaboration which we saw so well developed in John's Gospel. In the latter case, of course, it remains probable that it still reflects Jesus' own understanding of his relationship with God as something distinctively intimate. But that conclusion we have already been able to draw from the examination of Jesus' use of 'Abba'.

Since our concern is to show *what* New Testament scholars conclude about Jesus, and *why*, it would probably be better to refrain from going further into the more disputed territory. The case has been sufficiently clear and the conclusion firm. Although John's Gospel is a well developed portrayal of Jesus' claims to divine sonship, that claim is in fact well rooted in Jesus' own ministry, and particularly in his prayer address to God as 'Abba'. Jesus, we may say with confidence, thought of himself as God's son and encouraged his disciples to share his own intimate relationship with God as his son.

The Uniqueness of the Title 'Son'

We should not end before we have noted just one further complication. It arises from the fact that we come to the New Testament evidence with the hindsight of nearly twenty centuries of Christian faith in Jesus as 'the Son of God'. For Christians 'Son of God' is a unique title. Only Jesus can be called 'the Son of God'. What we must realize, however, is that there was nothing particularly unique about calling someone 'son of God' at the time of Jesus. Indeed in the period in which Christianity began many people were regarded as sons of God – that is, as enjoying the favour or approval or authorization of God. Oriental rulers, particularly in Egypt, were called sons of God – a title occasionally applied to the Jewish king as well (as in II Sam. 7.14). Outside Judaism famous philosophers like Pythagoras and Plato were sometimes spoken of as having been begotten by a god (Apollo). Israel itself is quite often spoken of as God's 'first-born son' (as in Ex. 4.22). Within Judaism, as *Jesus: the Evidence* rightly noted, there were at least two charismatic rabbis from around the time of Jesus who are remembered as having enjoyed a relationship of sonship before God as Father. And of wider application, 'the righteous man' was quite often spoken of as God's son. Consider, for example, the Wisdom of Solomon, a book probably written in the century before Jesus. In chapter 2.13–18 the enemies of the righteous man are depicted as speaking:

> Let us lie in wait for the righteous man,
> because he is inconvenient to us and opposes our actions;
> he reproaches us for sins against the law,
> and accuses us of sins against our training.
> He professes to have knowledge of God,
> and calls himself a child of the Lord. . . .
> he calls the last end of the righteous happy,
> and boasts that God is his father.
> Let us see if his words are true, . . .
> for if the righteous man is God's son, he will help him,
> and he will deliver him from the hand of his adversaries.

The degree of intimacy may not be the same as with Jesus' use of 'Abba'. But the point remains that when Christians called Jesus God's son they would not have been heard as making the same exclusive claim for Jesus' uniqueness which the title 'Son of God' has in application to Jesus now. This is one of the reasons why it would be unwise to argue about whether a capital letter (Son or son) is appropriate for Jesus' own self-understanding or for the first stages of Christian belief in Jesus as God's son/Son.

This observation, however, should not be seen as lessening the Christian claim for the significance of Jesus. On the contrary, it helps to highlight the significance which the first Christians did in the event recognize in Jesus. For it was not the application of the *title* 'Son of God' to Jesus which transformed Jesus from someone rather ordinary to someone unique. 'Son of God' was too common a description for that. On the contrary, it was the distinctiveness of *Jesus* which caused a rather more commonplace title to gain its note of exclusiveness, because it had been applied to him! Not a unique claim made Jesus appear unique; but by its application to him 'Son of God' came to signify the uniqueness which characterized Jesus' relationship to God.

Note on Professor Smith's View

The second programme in the series *Jesus: the Evidence* gave prominence to the views of Professor Morton Smith of Columbia University,
New York. In 1958 Professor Smith himself discovered a letter
claiming to be the work of Clement of Alexandria (who flourished
between AD 180 and 200). In this letter there is talk of a secret Gospel
of Mark which tells of a young man coming to Jesus and staying with
him through the night while Jesus taught him 'the mystery of the
kingdom'. Professor Smith infers from this that Jesus probably practised some secret nocturnal initiation.

1. On the basis of seeing a transcription of the text most scholars
have accepted that the text is from Clement. Though until more
experts have been able to examine and subject the original to appropriate tests the possibility of some elaborate hoax cannot finally be
ruled out. This point is made also in the notes accompanying Professor
Smith's photograph of the letter in Ian Wilson's *Jesus: the Evidence*,
written to accompany the television series.

2. The episode in which the visit of the young man is recorded
can be readily explained as a reworked amalgam of elements from
Mark 10 (the rich man, and Bartimaeus, principally) and the
story of Lazarus in John 11. There is nothing in the text itself to
indicate that the episode is an earlier version of accounts in Mark
and John.

3. As the letter itself states, the text of the secret Gospel comes
from the Carpocratians, who claimed to be custodians of secret
teaching from Jesus, and who may well have used the claim to justify
a degree of sexual licence in their esoteric practices. Such claims
were not uncommon among second-century groups who drew upon
Christian tradition and elaborated it for their own purposes. If auth-
entic, the letter of Clement probably refers to such elaboration. In
the letter itself Clement accepts that the secret Gospel was written
by Mark; but Clement is well known for his uncritical acceptance of
a wide range of material beyond the New Testament.

4. Professor Smith's elaboration of his thesis becomes increasingly
fanciful – particularly his suggestion that in his secret nocturnal
initiation Jesus may have given the initiates a hypnotic experience in
which they shared his ascent to the kingdom of heaven (based on the
story of the Transfiguration in Mark 9). No wonder Professor Henry
Chadwick of Cambridge University, in the follow-up discussion

programme, described Professor Smith's view as 'marvellously implausible, delightful to read; and there is not the slightest chance that it is true'.

3 What did the First Christians Believe about the Resurrection?

A third area of tension between historical research and Christian faith exposed to view by *Jesus: the Evidence* concerns the resurrection of Jesus. According to the third programme in the series, modern scholarship presents a very different view of the evidence on which is based the Christian belief that God raised Jesus from the dead. There was nothing unusual in the 'resurrection appearances'; there are numerous reports of appearances of divine figures like Isis and Asclepius (two of the most popular deities of that period). And the stories of the empty tomb may not have emerged for some years or even decades after the death of Jesus. Indeed, according to one New Testament scholar much featured in the third programme (Professor H. Koester of Harvard University), they can only have arisen when Christians fled from Jerusalem, shortly before AD 66. Since they could no longer worship at the tomb of Jesus (as must have been their practice till then), the story of the tomb being empty was put about as a way of explaining the lack of worship at Jesus' tomb. Quite where this left Christian belief in the resurrection was a point never developed.

Here again the programme touched a sensitive nerve for many if not most Christians. The belief that God raised Jesus from the dead is, if anything, of even more fundamental importance to Christian faith than the belief in Jesus as the Son of God. If it is untrue, or true only in a very vague sense, a whole range of basic Christian doctrines would have to be rewritten – particularly Christian understanding of who Jesus was and is, of the significance and effectiveness of his death, and of the hope which Christians entertain for themselves and for humanity. The words of Paul to the church in Corinth are often quoted in this connection, and with justification: 'If Christ has not been raised, your faith is futile and you are still in your sins' (I Cor. 15.17).

The question therefore is as important as any question can be for Christians: Has modern scholarship disproved the resurrection? Or expressed more carefully, Has modern scholarship made belief in the

resurrection of Jesus more difficult? To answer immediately, Yes and
No, as we have been able to do in the preceding chapters, is less
appropriate in this case. The issues here are more complex than can
be stated in a brief opening sentence. So we must start by stepping
back from the question in order to gain a clearer view of it – a clearer
view of the question itself and of why it is a question.

The Task of Historical Reconstruction

The task of the historian is a difficult one at any time. To do his job
properly he has to make some distinction along the following lines:
a distinction between *event*, *data* and *reconstructed event*.

The most important thing about the *event* is that it is past and gone.
It can never be experienced again. An event like it can be experienced
now or in the future. The memory of the event may still be cherished
in the present. But the event itself cannot be re-encountered. In its
uniqueness as an event it is unrepeatable. This obviously has
immediate consequences for the historian who is interested in an
event of the past (whether in a single event or one of a sequence of
events is irrelevant for our present discussion). For it simply means
that his investigation of that event is inevitably limited to some extent
at least – limited by the fact that he cannot experience that event for
himself. He has no immediate access to that event. He was not there.
He was not part of the event with all the questions he wants to find
answers for now.

But of course he is not entirely cut off from the event. He has no
access to the event itself. But he does have access to various *data*
which link him to the event. Whether the link is strong or weak
depends on the quality of the data. The data will usually include
people and things involved in the event, eyewitnesses, written reports,
circumstantial evidence, and so on. The closer in time he is to the
event, the closer he will be to the event. Through firsthand reports
etc. he will be at only one remove from the event. Conversely, the
farther back in time the event is, the further he will be from the
event. He will not be able to cross-examine eyewitnesses. Written
records, archaeological finds, and so forth, may not provide answers
to the questions he is asking. But usually there will be *some* data
which will provide *some* link to the event. Without such a link his
task as a historian would be impossible.

The historian's task is to use what data he has to *reconstruct what
he thinks happened*. He has no delusions about that task. He knows
full well that the reconstructed event can never be a precise reproduction of the event. The data is never enough. The reconstructed
event will always be an approximation to the event. The fuller the

data, the better his chances that the reconstruction will be a close approximation to the event. The less adequate the data, the more difficult his chances of reconstructing something which is reasonably approximate to what in the event happened.

The difficulty of the historian's task has several aspects. Let me simply mention two of the most important. In the first place, only rarely is an 'event' straightforwardly objective. Events are experienced by those involved in them. And, of course, they are experienced differently. So when we talk of a historical event, what we are usually talking about is the event as it was experienced by this person or that. Even when events are strictly objective, their objectivity is not usually the most important aspect of them. Julius Caesar crossed the Rubicon on 10 January 49 BC. That is the objective event. But much more important is the question of how that event was perceived by Caesar and by his opponents. In many cases it would be more accurate to speak of many events rather than one event, since the participants and eyewitnesses of the event perceived it differently.

A second difficulty has already been hinted at – the need for the historian to cross-examine the data. He must take account of the bias of the written record, the chance factors which have preserved some evidence and not others, the unstated assumptions of his source which did not need to be stated because everyone took them for granted at the time, and so on. The data are rarely simple 'raw' data. They have already been 'cooked' to one degree or other. To change the metaphor, they have been filtered through the medium or media through which they reached the historian. He must always ask, How much has been filtered out? How much have they been 'contaminated' by the medium?

All this means that the use of historical data to reconstruct historical events is a very skilled job. The historian must *interpret* his data in order to achieve the most satisfactory reconstruction. He must allow for distortion in the data and bias in himself. And there will always be something tentative or provisional about his reconstruction, since there is always the possibility that new data will emerge which will require a realignment of other data and a reassessment of the reconstructed event.

This may sound exceedingly complex and demanding, and the task of reconstruction so difficult as to be well-nigh impossible. But of course, all that I have said so far could be taken as a description of the task of a trial jury. They too are separate from the event. The task of the counsels for defence and prosecution is to present all the relevant data, and through cross-examination to present the reconstruction of the event most favourable to their case. The jury must interpret the data for themselves, allowing for the limitations of witnesses' testimony and the special pleading of barristers. And in the end of the day they must decide which reconstruction of the event is closest to the event – the prosecution's, the defence's, or their own. There does not have to be a perfect match between reconstructed event and event. There can be a number of loose ends, data which do not entirely fit. But so long as they are confident that the prosecution's reconstruction is reasonably close to the event ('beyond reasonable doubt') they are duty-bound to convict.

In principle the historian's task is the same. With events far back in history the data are less and the reconstruction more difficult and usually less certain. But the task is essentially the same. What then about the case before us now – the resurrection of Jesus from the dead? or to retain the analogy, the Christian allegation that Jesus was raised from the dead?

The Data Concerning 'the Resurrection of Jesus'

If the event in question is 'the resurrection of Jesus', then we must start with the recognition that we cannot get back directly to it. Even if Christians claim to encounter Jesus Christ alive now, that is not the same thing: whatever or whoever they are experiencing, it is not the resurrection of Jesus itself. That belongs to the irretrievable pastness of history. As usual, all we have is data. In this case we may group the data into five categories. To begin with I will simply list the data. The cross-examination will follow.

Reports of Jesus' tomb being found empty

These occur in all four Gospels. The first three can again be represented in parallel – Matt. 28, Mark 16 and Luke 24.

THE EMPTY TOMB

Matt. 28.1–10	Mark 16.1–8	Luke 24.1–11 (12)
[1] Now after the sabbath, toward the dawn of the first day of the week, Mary Magdalene and the other Mary went to see the sepulchre.	[1] And when the sabbath was past, Mary Magdalene, and Mary the mother of James, and Salome, bought spices, so that they might go and anoint him. [2] And very early on the first day of the week they went to the tomb when the sun had risen.	[1] But on the first day of the week, at early dawn, they went to the tomb, taking the spices which they had prepared.

2 And behold, there was a great earthquake; for an angel of the Lord descended from heaven and came and rolled back the stone, and sat upon it. 3 His appearance was like lightning, and his raiment white as snow. 4 And for fear of him the guards trembled and became like dead men.

3 And they were saying to one another, 'Who will roll away the stone for us from the door of the tomb?' 4 And looking up, they saw that the stone was rolled back; for it was very large. 5 And entering the tomb,

2 And they found the stone rolled away from the tomb, 3 but when they went in they did not find the body. 4 While they were perplexed about this, behold, two men stood by them in dazzling apparel; 5 and as they were frightened and bowed their faces to the ground, the men said to them, 'Why do you seek the living among the dead?

they saw a young man sitting on the right side, dressed in a white robe; and they were amazed. 6 And he said to them, 'Do not be amazed; you seek Jesus of Nazareth, who was crucified. He has risen, he is not here; see the place where they laid him. 7 But go, tell his disciples and Peter

5 But the angel said to the women, 'Do not be afraid; for I know that you seek Jesus who was crucified. 6 He is not here; for he has risen, as he said. Come, see the place where he lay. 7 Then go quickly and tell his disciples that he has risen from the dead, and behold, he is going before you to Galilee; there you will see him. Lo, I have told you.'

that he is going before you to Galilee; there you will see him, as he told you.'

6 Remember how he told you while he was still in Galilee, 7 that the Son of man must be delivered into the hands of sinful men, and be crucified, and on the third day rise.' 8 And they remembered his words, 9 and returning from the tomb they told all this to the eleven and to all the rest.

8 So they departed quickly from the tomb with fear and great joy, and ran to tell his disciples.

8 And they went out and fled from the tomb; for trembling and astonishment had come upon them; and they said nothing to any one, for they were afraid.

The account in John is close to the others to start with, but then provides a different version – John 20.1–10.

Now on the first day of the week Mary Magdalene came to the tomb early, while it was still dark, and saw that the stone had been taken away from the tomb. So she ran, and went to Simon Peter and the other disciple, the one whom Jesus loved, and said to them, 'They have taken the Lord out of the tomb, and we do not know where they have laid him'. Peter then came out with the other disciple, and they went toward the tomb. They both ran, but the other disciple outran Peter and reached the tomb first; and stooping to look in, he saw the linen cloths lying there, but he did not go in. Then Simon Peter came, following him, and went into the tomb; he saw the linen cloths lying, and the napkin, which had been on his head, not lying with the linen cloths but rolled up in a place by itself. Then the other disciple, who reached the tomb first, also went in, and he saw and believed; for as yet they did not know the scripture, that he must rise from the dead. Then the disciples went back to their homes.

Reported 'sightings' of Jesus after his death

To avoid prejudging the data I use the neutral word 'sighting'. Matthew records two such sightings: Matt. 28.8–10,16–20. The first picks up where the story left off in the Synoptic presentation above.

[The women] departed quickly from the tomb with fear and great joy, and ran to tell his disciples. And behold, Jesus met them and said, 'Hail!'. And they came up and took hold of his feet and worshipped him. Then Jesus said to them, 'Do not be afraid; go and tell my brethren to go to Galilee, and there they will see me'.

A few verses later Matthew concludes his Gospel.

Now the eleven disciples went to Galilee, to the mountain to which Jesus had directed them. And when they saw him they worshiped him; but some doubted. And Jesus came and said to them, 'All authority in heaven and on earth has been given to me. Go therefore and make disciples . . .'.

The earliest texts of Mark do not have any 'sightings'; they end at verse 8, and Mark may indeed have intended to end there. The longer ending (verses 9–20) was certainly added at a later date to round Mark's narrative off in a way which later scribes and teachers regarded as more fitting.

Luke 24.13–35 gives the lengthy account of the two disciples encountering Jesus on the road to Emmaus. At the end of that story, when the two return to Jerusalem, an earlier appearance to Peter is mentioned: 'The Lord has risen indeed, and has appeared to Simon' (24.34). It is followed by a further appearance to the disciples as a group – Luke 24.36–43.

As they were saying this, Jesus himself stood among them. But they were startled and frightened, and supposed that they saw a spirit. And he said to them. 'Why are you troubled, and why do questionings rise in your hearts? See my hands and my feet, that it is I myself; handle me, and see; for a spirit has not flesh and bones as you see that I have.' And while they still disbelieved for joy, and wondered, he said to them, 'Have you anything here to eat?'. They gave him a piece of broiled fish, and he took it and ate before them.

Luke's Gospel concludes with a brief account of Jesus being taken to heaven after commissioning the disciples. Luke's second volume (the Acts of the Apostles) speaks of further appearings prior to his being taken up to heaven (Acts 1.1–11).

John's Gospel has the most extensive sequence of 'sightings' – to Mary Magdalene at the tomb, when she mistakes Jesus for the gardener (John 20.11–18), the same evening to the disciples when Thomas is absent (20.19–23), a week later to Thomas in the presence of the other disciples (20.24–29), and finally to seven of the disciples in Galilee, in what gives the impression of being an appendix to the Gospel (21.1–23).

In the case of the 'appearances' however, we also have testimony from outside the circle of the Gospel writers. For Paul too speaks of various sightings. He gives no account of them, but lists at least six appearances in his first letter to the church in Corinth – I Cor. 15.3–8.

> I delivered to you as of first importance what I also received, that Christ died for our sins in accordance with the scriptures, that he was buried, that he was raised on the third day in accordance with the scriptures, and that he appeared to Cephas, then to the twelve. Then he appeared to more than five hundred brethren at one time, most of whom are still alive, though some have fallen asleep. Then he appeared to James, then to all the apostles. Last of all, as to one untimely born, he appeared also to me.

Transformation of the first disciples and initial spread of the new faith

With this data we move from more direct evidence to circumstantial evidence. What is in view here in the first place is the marked 'before and after' difference in the disciples. Before the event ('the resurrection of Jesus'), the Gospels depict the disciples as demoralized and broken. They had abandoned Jesus and fled when he was arrested in the garden called Gethsemane (Mark 14.50). Peter had tried to stay close but on being challenged had disowned Jesus completely (Mark 15.66–72). Only women and lesser known disciples are represented as remaining loyal when Jesus is on the cross and as having a care for his corpse (Mark 15.40–16.1). The two disciples on the road to Emmaus lament over their shattered hopes – 'We had hoped that he was the one to redeem Israel' (Luke 24.21). In the appendix to John's Gospel the disciples have returned to Galilee and seem to lack any sense of purpose or direction (John 21.2–3).

Contrast the picture of the same disciples in the early chapters of Acts. Peter and John move among the people of Jerusalem bearing

witness to their faith in Jesus quite openly. When summoned before
the highest court in the land they speak so fearlessly that the court
is surprised: 'When they saw the boldness of Peter and John, and
perceived that they were uneducated, common men, they wondered'
(Acts 4.13). When the court orders them to cease speaking or
teaching in the name of Jesus, Peter and John reply, 'Whether it is
right in the sight of God, you must judge; for we cannot but speak
of what we have seen and heard' (4.19–20). On being released and
returning to their friends, they receive fresh inspiration and speak
out with still more boldness (4.31).

Such testimony would, of course, have to be cross-examined and
its value assessed. But on first reading there is certainly relevant
testimony here. If men were transformed from frightened men
cowering indoors 'for fear of the Jews' (John 20.19) to men who
could not be intimidated even by the leading Jewish authorities,
something must have happened to them. There must be an adequate
explanation for such an outcome. 'The resurrection of Jesus' is part
of that explanation in the Christian sources.

The evidence of the initial spread of Christianity is simply an exten-
sion of the same range of data. The Acts of the Apostles depicts a
very rapid growth – 3,000 baptized on the day of Pentecost (Acts
2.41), soon growing to about 5,000 (4.4). Later on we read of 'many
thousands among the Jews who have believed' (21.20). There was
certainly a very rapid growth among Gentiles (non-Jews), so much
so that within a hundred years Christianity seems to have become
predominantly Gentile in membership (see further chapter 4). More
striking still is the fact that within three hundred years of Christianity's
being founded, and despite years of fierce persecution, it had become
the state religion of the Roman Empire.

Here too we have a sequence of events of undoubted significance.
The counsel for Christianity would want to argue that such a sequence
requires a starting event of sufficient significance to explain what
followed. The value of circumstantial evidence is that it calls for
an explanation of that evidence. Whatever fits best with the set of
circumstances indicated by the data is likely to be the best reconstruction of the event which gave rise to the data. From the Christian
perspective 'the resurrection of Jesus' is a central part of that explanation. At the same time Christians should bear in mind that this
particular argument is a two-edged weapon. For, if anything, the
initial spread of Islam in the seventh and eighth centuries was *more*
dramatic and spectacular!

The very high estimate of Jesus which soon became established in Christian faith

Here the data focusses on the striking fact that within a few years the first Christians were speaking about Jesus in divine terms. The most outspoken testimony comes from John's Gospel. It begins by speaking of 'the Word' which/who was in the beginning with God and was God, through which/whom 'all things were made', and which/who became flesh in Jesus Christ (John 1.1–3, 14). The prologue to the Gospel ends by calling Jesus 'the only Son', or 'the only-begotten God' (1.18); there are different readings in the ancient Greek manuscripts, but the latter is more likely. In the same vein the Gospel reaches its climax in the adoring confession of Thomas, 'My Lord and my God!' (20.28). In addition we may simply recall the very high view of Jesus presented by John the Evangelist (above chapter 2). The probability that this is a developed view (chapter 2) is of no consequence here. It is the fact of such a development within seventy years of Jesus' ministry which is so striking.

But already within the first generation of Christianity we see Jesus being spoken of in divine terms. Whether he is called 'god' in Romans 9.5 is not finally clear from the text. But he is called 'Lord' all the time by Paul. The significance of that title emerges when we recall that 'Lord' was the way of referring to *God* among the Greek-speaking Jews of Paul's time, at least those with whom Paul had to deal. How much weight Paul puts upon this title is indicated by another verse in Romans – 'Everyone who calls upon the name of the Lord will be saved' (10.13). In the context it is clear that 'the Lord' is Jesus (10.9). But verse 13 is actually a quotation from the Old Testament (Joel 2.32), where 'the Lord' is God himself. Presumably then there is some merging of God and Jesus or at least of their functions in Paul's view.

This evidence (and we have cited only part of it) should not be overvalued. To feel the weight of its testimony we would have to recall that in the ancient world it was by no means unknown for famous men (kings, heroes of the faith, philosophers) to be thought of as deified after death (see below p. 71). But neither should the data here be *under*valued. For the testimony comes not from Gentiles to whom the deification of an emperor was more like a promotion to 'the upper chamber'. It comes from Jews. And Jews were the most fiercely monotheistic race of that age. So resolute was their insistance that God is one and beside him is no other, that they were often regarded as atheists! – because they refused to acknowledge that their God was just one God among others, or one way of speaking of a God whom they in fact shared with others. For a *Jew* to speak of a *man*, Jesus, in terms which showed him as sharing in the deity of *God*, was a quite astonishing feature of earliest Christianity.

Perhaps the most striking passage of all at this point is Philippians 2.9–11: '. . . at the name of Jesus every knee should bow, . . . and every tongue confess that Jesus Christ is Lord . . .'. What is so striking is that it clearly alludes to Isaiah 45.23: 'to me every knee shall bow, every tongue shall swear'. And that comes as part of one of the strongest monotheistic assertions of the Old Testament – '. . . I am God, and there is no other . . .' (Isa. 45.22). The 'me' of v.23 is the one God, beside whom there is none other. And yet, Paul refers the passage to *Jesus*. In other words, within thirty years or so of Jesus' death, Jesus was being spoken of in terms that indicate that a radical revolution was already underway in the Jewish conception of God.

If then we are in the business of tracing chains of cause and effect, we have to recognize here a very significant 'effect'. An important part of weighing the evidence will be checking whether we can uncover a sufficient cause to explain that effect. From the Christian perspective a fundamental part of the cause must be 'the resurrection of Jesus'. For Paul the Christian, confession of Jesus as Lord evidently arose out of belief that God raised Jesus from the dead (Rom. 10.9).

Claims of believers since the beginning of Christianity to encounter Jesus alive here and now

Many Christians would want to include within the basic data the testimony of believers today. 'I know that Jesus is alive. I was speaking to him this morning.'

In a full-scale evaluation of the evidence such testimonies would have to be examined with care. Their potential value is considerable. The personal experience of a witness has more immediacy and directness than any of the other data so far listed.

We, however, will have to pass over this evidence. For such testimonies are rarely, if ever, of independent value. They almost always depend to an important extent on the prior beliefs outlined in the preceding paragraphs. It is because the Christian already believes that Jesus is alive from the dead that he can recognize his experience in prayer or devotion as an encounter with Jesus. Because he believes that the resurrection of Jesus was the critical point of the ignition sequence which blasted Christian understanding of Jesus skyward and which made Christianity itself 'take off', he can also believe that as a Christian he is in communication with this Jesus. I do not mean that such testimonies are invalid or are necessarily to be discounted. I simply make the point that they are at least to some extent secondary to the earlier beliefs. Any cross-examination would have to evaluate the earlier beliefs before reaching a firm conclusion about the weight to be attached to such testimonies. In the limited space available to us here we must focus our attention on the evidence which is most central in the inquiry.

The same is true in some measure of the data outlined in the two preceding subsections (transformation of disciples, and high estimate of Jesus). It was in part at least because the first Christians believed that God had raised Jesus from the dead that they could preach and evangelize with such boldness. And their reassessment of the true significance of Jesus sprang in large measure from the same source. Belief in the resurrection itself derived if anything from the first two collections of data – the empty tomb reports and the 'sightings' of Jesus. That belief was a powerful catalyst which helped set in train the transformation in the disciples and in their understanding of Christ. To acknowledge this is not to reduce the other data to the status of a mere corollary of the prior belief in the resurrection. It is simply to point out that if we wish to clarify the basic belief in the resurrection of Jesus, our primary (and in this chapter exclusive) attention will have to be given to the most central data – the reports of the empty tomb and the reported sightings of Jesus after his death.

Even here our task will have to be limited. To subject this data to a proper cross-examination would require more time and detailed argument than is suitable for our present purposes. We must be content to indicate briefly the scope of the discussion, and particularly the considerations which weigh most heavily with Christian scholars when they find that the evidence calls for positive assessment.

The Empty Tomb

We look first at the reports of Jesus' tomb being found empty.

Conflicting evidence

Any jury scrutinizing the data listed above under this heading would have to take account of the several differences between the four Gospel narratives. The most important can be listed briefly.

1. The number of women involved – two (Matt.), three (Mark) or one (John)?

2. The timing – before dawn (Matt., John) or after dawn (Mark)?

3. Was the stone rolled back in the presence of the women (as Matthew may imply) or before they reached the tomb (Mark, Luke, John)?

4. Was there a communication on the first visit to the tomb (Matt., Mark, Luke) or not (John)?

5. How many angels – one (Matt., Mark), two (Luke), none (John)?

6. Did the women tell the other disciples (Matt., Luke, John) or not (Mark)?

There are also distinctive features in Matthew (the guard at the tomb – Matt. 27.62–66; 28.4) and in John (the involvement of Peter and the beloved disciple – John 20.2–10).

It can hardly be denied that here we have conflict of testimony. There is nothing surprising in this. Conflict of testimony occurs in all trials to some extent. Some may be the result of false testimony. But it will be impossible to eliminate all conflict. As we noted above (p. 55), an event is experienced differently by the different participants. So their different accounts of it will not always mesh together into a single whole. Consequently a jury considering the data regarding the alleged empty tomb would have to ask, Does the degree of conflict here go beyond what one might expect when dealing with different testimonies to the same event? In particular, is the degree of confusion more or less than we might expect where the participants were very emotionally involved?

Moreover, our earlier discussion provokes a further question. Is the amount of disagreement significantly different from the amount of disagreement between other Gospel accounts of the same event? We noted in chapter 1 how narratives could diverge even when they were clearly recounting the same basic story. Another example would be the healing of a blind man (or was it two blind men?) on the way into (or was it out of?) Jericho (Matt. 20.29–30; Mark 10.46; Luke 18.35). The best example of how far accounts of the same event can diverge in the process of retelling is the death of Judas. We may be sure it was the same event (Judas died only once!), and some associated details are clear (use of the blood money to buy 'Blood Field'). But what precisely happened is now almost impossible to discern (Matt. 27.3–10; Acts 1.18–19). How many of the divergences in the accounts of the empty tomb are the result of varying emphases and embellishments of a basic account underlying them all?

Under such questioning the importance of the *conflict* of testimony becomes less weighty. And the point on which they all agree if anything gains greater significance. The unanimity of the claim that the tomb was empty remains an impressive datum.

We have not yet mentioned one other potential conflict – between Paul on the one hand and the united testimony of the Gospels. It remains a somewhat uncomfortable fact that Paul nowhere mentions the tomb of Jesus being empty, not even in that outline of the basic gospel which he himself had received at the beginning of his life as a Christian. To be sure, he mentions Jesus' being buried (I Cor. 15.4). But in the idiom of his time that could simply be a way of emphasizing that Jesus was really dead (cf. Rom. 6.4). There is, however, a question to be asked here: How relevant was the emptiness (or otherwise) of the tomb to Paul's treatment in I Cor. 15? This is a question to which we can return later, with greater benefit. For the moment we may simply note that Paul does not actually address the issue of the empty tomb. His silence on the subject is somewhat surprising, but does not necessarily count against the unanimous testimony of the Gospels.

Considerations in favour

A number of factors combine to strengthen the case for accepting the Gospels' testimony regarding the emptiness of Jesus' tomb. Indeed the strength of the arguments in favour of seeing the emptiness of Jesus' tomb as a piece of factual historical information is often not appreciated, even among Christians. In this case scholarship should be credited with uncovering several factors which together build up into an impressive case.

1. Notice first that all four Gospels attribute the discovery of the tomb's emptiness to *women*. In our day, accustomed as we are to the drive for sexual equality, that may not seem anything out of the ordinary. But in the Palestine of that time a woman's status and testimony was not as highly regarded as a man's. Indeed, women were probably regarded as unreliable witnesses in first-century Judaism, simply because they were women. A recent announcement in Iran ruled that a woman's testimony was only half the value of a man's. A very similar attitude was dominant in the eastern end of the Mediterranean at the time of Jesus. That being so, we must conclude that a testimony in which women are presented as the primary witnesses must be based on sound fact. A contrived narrative would hardly have given the leading testimony to women. Why attribute it to women? Who would believe that? The only good reason for attributing the report of the empty tomb to women is that this was the way it was remembered as having actually happened.

2. The confusion between the different accounts in the Gospels does not appear to have been contrived. The conflict of testimony is more a mark of the sincerity of those from whom the testimony was derived than a mark against their veracity. We may judge the witnesses to be confused on points of detail (as witnesses often are when they try to recall particular details), but hardly deceptive. And to describe them as untrustworthy on the basis of such differences

would be ungenerous. On the contrary, the more unanimous the testimony at all points of detail, the more we would be forced to conclude that they had all derived their testimony from a single source. In which case we would no longer have four testimonies but one testimony. But in the Gospels we must speak of at least two or three different accounts, whose measure of agreement and disagreement is sufficient to give weight to their united testimony.

Worth noting in particular is the surprising character of what is probably the earliest of the four Gospels – Mark. If indeed the original text did end at verse 8 of chapter 16, as is quite probable, it would mean that the evangelist ended with the witnesses to the empty tomb too afraid to say anything. Certainly there is a nice dramatic sense here – the evangelist deliberately leaving unresolved the disharmony caused by the final note of fear. But even so, it has what J. B. Phillips calls 'the ring of truth' – not least in the implication that the sign of the empty tomb is somewhat ambiguous: it was not immediately understood as evidence for resurrection.

Moreover, the fact that the earliest Gospel (Mark) ends without any record of a 'resurrection appearance', has to be matched with the fact that the earliest account of 'resurrection appearances' (I Cor. 15) has no reference to the tomb being empty. This degree of independence and lack of correlation between the two earliest records speaks favourably for the value of each. There is nothing to indicate that one was contrived to bolster the other.

3. Somewhat surprisingly there is archaeological evidence which indirectly but quite strongly suggests that the tomb must have been empty. Burial practice is, of course, one of the customs on which archaeology can often speak with great authority. In this case we know that at the time of Jesus it had become customary to return to the tomb where a loved one had been laid, after a sufficient period had elapsed (a year), to gather up the bones and put them in a bone box (ossuary). The reasoning was straightforward: the bones should be kept together so that in the resurrection God could use them to (re)construct the body for resurrection. The bones would provide the framework on which God could reconstitute the body – the process described, in fact, in Ezekiel's famous vision of the valley of dry bones (Ezek. 37.7–10). At a later date, after discussion on the subject, the rabbis concluded that God did not need the whole skeletal remains. One bone would be sufficient.

The point is this. Archaeology has now provided evidence that at the time of Jesus a popular understanding of resurrection in Palestine would have involved some 're-use' of the dead body. That this was indeed a popular view at the period with which we are concerned, is confirmed by two passages in the New Testament, which seem to reflect the same popular view – Matt. 27.52–53 and John 5.28–29. In both cases the talk is of resurrection as the dead, or the bodies of the dead, 'coming out of the tombs'.

It follows that in Palestine the ideas of resurrection and of empty tomb would naturally go together for many people. But this also means that any assertion that Jesus had been raised would be unlikely to cut much ice *unless his tomb was empty*. A claim made in Jerusalem within a few weeks of his crucifixion, that God had raised Jesus (that is, the body of Jesus) from death, would not have gained much credence had his tomb been undisturbed or the fate of his body known to be otherwise. The absence of any such counter claim in any available literature of the period (Christian or Jewish) is therefore important. The one exception, if 'exception' is the right word, is Matt. 28.13–15 – the attempt of the Jewish authorities to put the story about that 'Jesus' disciples came by night and stole him away'. How far back the account goes is debated. But at least it is clear that at the time of Matthew this explanation was current among the Jews (28.15). The significance is clear: even a Jewish response to the Christian claim did not dispute the testimony about the tomb being empty; on the contrary, the emptiness of the tomb was not a point of controversy, only the explanation of why it was empty.

4. A further strong consideration in favour of the empty tomb reports being regarded as rooted in historical fact is the absence of any tomb veneration in earliest Christianity. We know that it was quite customary at the time of Jesus for devotees to meet at the tomb of the dead prophet for worship. The practice is reflected in Matt. 23.29 ('you build the tombs of the prophets and adorn the monuments of the righteous'). And it continues today in the veneration accorded to the tombs of Abraham in Hebron and of David in Jerusalem. *Jesus: the Evidence* provided fascinating footage of the worship still practised at the tomb of the lesser known near contemporary of Jesus, the charismatic rabbi, Honi, 'the circle-drawer'.

Christians today of course regard the site of Jesus' tomb with similar veneration, and that practice goes back at least to the fourth century. But for the period covered by the New Testament and other earliest Christian writings there is no evidence whatsoever for Christians regarding the place where Jesus had been buried as having any special significance. *No* practice of tomb veneration, or even of meeting for worship at Jesus' tomb is attested for the first Christians. Had such been the practice of the first Christians, with all the significance which the very practice itself presupposes, it is hard to believe that our records of Jerusalem Christianity and of Christian visits thereto would not have mentioned or alluded to it in some way or at some point.

This strange silence, exceptional in view of the religious practice of the time, has only one obvious explanation. The first Christians did not regard the place where Jesus had been laid as having any special significance because no grave was thought to contain Jesus' earthly remains. The tomb was not venerated, it did not become a place of pilgrimage, because the tomb was empty!

Conclusions

The testimony is of course fragmentary. A jury would require a good deal more before it could reach a verdict 'beyond reasonable doubt'. But if we have to draw conclusions on the basis of the evidence available to us, I have to say quite forcefully: the probability is that the tomb was empty. As a matter of historical reconstruction, the weight of evidence points firmly to the conclusion that Jesus' tomb was found empty and that its emptiness was a factor in the first Christians' belief in the resurrection of Jesus.

The chief alternative interpretations of the data all seem to me, and in the view of many scholars, to involve greater improbabilities. The suggestion that the body had in fact been left undisturbed, or that others had stolen it makes hard work of the third consideration above. Had the fate of Jesus' body been known to rule out the claim that God had 're-used' it, it is hard to understand how and why the Christian claim went unchallenged. In the Palestine of that time nothing could have provided a more devastating rebuttal of the Christian claim than a testimony that Jesus' body or bones still lay in their final resting place.

The argument that the disciples themselves stole the body runs up against the fourth consideration above. Even if we suppose that only a few were involved in the conspiracy, it is hard to believe that no hint or rumour of it reached a larger body of disciples. And if some knew that Jesus' final tomb was *not* empty, it is even harder to believe that they did not make *that* tomb a place of pilgrimage. The duplicity involved, not only in proclaiming Jesus' resurrection when it was known that his bones were undisturbed, but also in failing to give due honour to the real tomb of the dead prophet, is hard to match with what we know of the first Christians.

A number of scholars do argue that the belief in an empty tomb arose late. For myself I find no evidence of this from the texts themselves; the data of the texts themselves are at best (or worst) ambiguous. But the other considerations mentioned above (1–4) seem to me to tip the balance of probability fairly heavily in favour of the historicity of the empty tomb. Professor Koester's rather idiosyncratic theory on the subject I will deal with in a little more detail at the end of the chapter

In short then, Christians should feel no embarrassment regarding the Gospels' report that Jesus' tomb was found empty. Some scholars question the report, but scholarship as a whole has done more to substantiate than to disprove it. Whatever we make of it, here, we may say with confidence, is a piece of good historical information.

Resurrection Appearances

The reports of Jesus' being seen alive after his death form the other set of primary data which call for scrutiny.

Conflicting evidence

Here too there is a certain amount of confusion. In particular, were there 'sightings' at or near the tomb (Matthew and John), or only later and elsewhere (as both Mark and Luke imply)? More important, were there appearances in Galilee (Matthew, Mark? and John) or only in Jerusalem (as Luke seems to indicate – Luke 24.49; Acts 1.4)? When we compare the four or five different sources of such reports (Matthew, Luke and Acts 1, John and I Cor. 15), a striking fact is the *lack* of parallel. Each contain one or more reports of which the others make no mention. Indeed, almost the only common ground between two or more is that (1) the earliest appearances were to women (Matthew and John), (2) one of the first appearances was to Peter (Luke 24.34; I Cor. 15.5), and (3) there was one or more appearances to 'the twelve' (all five, including Acts 1.2–3 and I Cor. 15.5).

Considerations in favour

In this case also there are various factors which indicate strongly that this testimony should not be lightly discounted as fabrication or cranky.

1. The earliest testimony goes back to a very early stage. Paul wrote his first letter to the Corinthians some time in the early 50s – between twenty and twenty-five years after the death of Jesus. That places it well within the life-time of many of those who claimed to have seen Jesus soon after his death. Indeed, Paul deliberately points out that many of the 'more than five hundred brethren' who saw Jesus 'are still alive' (15.6). The invitation is clear: we have plenty of firsthand witnesses; you can ask them yourselves. Paul evidently had no qualms about his witnesses being subjected to cross-examination.

Moreover, Paul explicitly states that the reports he outlines in I Cor. 15 he had himself received from those before him in believing in Christ (15.3). Paul was converted within two or three years of Jesus' death, perhaps as little as eighteen months after the first reports of Jesus being seen alive after his death. And almost certainly he received this basic outline of the gospel very soon after his conversion, as part of his initial instruction. In other words, the testimony of I Cor. 15.3–8 goes back to within two or three years of the events described. In terms of ancient reports about events in the distant past, we are much closer to eyewitness testimony than is usually the case.

2. Note again the prominence of women in the records of the first 'sightings' (Matt. 28; John 20). The significance of this factor I have already explained above (p. 65). The implication is the same in this case. Since women's testimony was not highly regarded in ancient Palestine, the most obvious explanation for the first reports being attributed to women is that in the actual event it was women who were the first to see Jesus.

Paul's omission of any women witnesses in his I Cor. 15 list may reflect something of the same bias. In what has the appearance of being a fairly formal list of witnesses, the inclusion of appearances to women would be regarded as a weakening of the claim not a strengthening. Contrariwise, the inclusion of such testimony else-where, *despite* the bias against women as witnesses, is all the more impressive.

3. In this case too there is no indication that the diversity of reports is contrived. There is a curious episodic character about the reports themselves and the way they are set down. Particularly in Matthew, Luke and John 21, there has been no real attempt to provide a coherent sequence or structured listing. Overall, the impression is given of a number of reported sightings which occurred on what might otherwise be called a random basis. This lack of artificiality again encourages a sympathetic assessment of the testimony being given. Naive we may think them, but not malicious or deceitful.

Worthy of particular mention is Matt. 28.17: 'When they saw him they worshipped him; but some doubted'. Here again we may speak of 'the ring of truth'. Of course the motif of doubt can often be introduced as a way of strengthening the claim being made. By showing that the doubt was resolved similar doubts on the part of the readers may be quietened. Both Luke and John make quite effective use of this technique (Luke 24.36–43; John 20.24–29), though in both cases they are probably working with already established tradition. But Matthew makes no attempt to show the doubt being resolved. Since, therefore, the note of doubt is not introduced in order to show how it was removed, the next best explanation is that it was intro-duced simply because it was part of the original eyewitness testimony.

In the event, some were not sure what to make of what they saw and experienced. As with Mark's account of the women returning from the tomb (Mark 16.8), so here. The witnesses admit that the events were of such a character that their response to them was somewhat confused. Where such honesty is evident in testimony, the calibre of that testimony, including the points of agreement, must be accorded high esteem.

Alternative explanations

Where the integrity of these early reports must be respected, the most obvious alternative explanation is that the witnesses were deluded – not deceitful, but deceived. In other words, the 'resurrection appearances' were in fact nothing more than hallucinatory projections of the first disciples' frustrated hopes, visions begotten of hysteria.

Here too, however, such a hypothesis runs into greater improbabilities than is often realized.

1. The parallel with visions of Isis and Asclepius (above p. 53) is hardly close. These were mythical figures from the dim past. In the sightings of Jesus we are talking about a man who had died only a few days or weeks earlier. Moreover, the psychological conditioning of those involved is different. Dreams of Asclepius were regularly expected as part of the healing process attributed to Asclepius. Indeed, at the temples dedicated to Asclepius there was normally a room set aside (an *abaton*) in which the god would appear to the patient in a healing dream. And in initiation ceremonies to the Isis cult visions were probably expected as the high point of the ceremony (there may be an allusion to this sort of belief in Col. 2.18). The situation with the first disciples was quite different. A much more complicated psychological process would have to be hypothesized to explain the first and subsequent seeings of Jesus. The more complicated, the more speculative. The more speculative, the more doubtful.

2. There are in fact much closer parallels if we want to draw them into the discussion. In the Jewish literature from this whole period we read of various visions of dead heroes of the faith (Abel, Jeremiah, 'the righteous man', among others). In these visions the individual is seen as robed in heavenly glory, a figure of majesty, numbered with the angels, or some such language. This seems to be a much better parallel. Until we realize that in no other case did the one(s) seeing the vision conclude, 'This man has been raised from the dead'. *It is not the seeing of Jesus after he was dead which was so surprising in the context of the times. It was the conclusion to which the seeing*

led which is without parallel. 'Visions' may be a quite appropriate
description of these 'sightings'. But they were visions of a peculiar
sort. Paul seems to be making just this point when he distinguishes
the resurrection appearances of I Cor. 15.3–8, which ended with
himself ('last of all'), from the various other visionary experiences he
knew thereafter (II Cor. 12.7). There was evidently a distinctiveness
about 'the resurrection appearances' which should not be lost sight
of in the search for parallels.

3. If we pursue the logic of the 'hallucinatory projection' explanation, we would expect the hallucinations to be made up of images
and symbols the first disciples had gleaned from Jesus. Of these the
image with greatest potential power to fire the imaginations of the
disappointed disciples would probably be the one of a heavenly figure
'coming on clouds of glory'. According to early traditions, the
disciples remembered Jesus as using just such language (especially
Mark 13.26; 14.62). Yet there is nothing of this in the various accounts
of resurrection appearances – even those where Jesus seems to appear
from heaven. For the rest, it is the unexpectedness of the manifest-
ation which is the stronger feature.

Here too, therefore, those offering the alternative explanations do
not seem to have probed the data with sufficient thoroughness. They
have allowed themselves to be impressed by parallels which, on closer
inspection, do not seem close enough to provide a satisfactory
analogy. There are uncharacteristic features in our accounts which
probably require an uncharacteristic explanation.

An odd belief

The most unusual feature is so unusual that it deserves separate
comment. I refer to *the oddness of the belief that Jesus had been
'raised from the dead'.* Christians and those well used to the Christian
tradition today are so familiar with this way of speaking about what
happened to Jesus after his death that they fail to realize just how
odd it was when first put forward, how strange the claim was when
it was first formulated. Two points should be noted.

1. There was a belief in resurrection at the time of Jesus. We know
that the Pharisees held such a belief (cf. Acts 23.6). And Jesus
evidently argued about it with the Sadducees (Mark 12.18–27). But
it was belief in the *final* resurrection. The resurrection the Pharisees
looked for was the resurrection of the dead at the end of history, the
'general resurrection' – the resurrection of which Daniel speaks:
'many of those who sleep in the dust of the earth shall awake, some
to everlasting life, and some to shame and everlasting contempt'

(Dan. 12.2). The unusual feature about the Christian claim was their belief that Jesus *alone* had been raised *before* the end.

2. More precisely, the first Christians believed that with Jesus' resurrection the *general* resurrection had *already begun*. In Romans 1.4 the phrase used for Jesus' resurrection is not, as we might expect, '*his* resurrection *from* the dead' (the more usual formulation), but '*the* resurrection *of* the dead'. Paul here probably quotes an older formula which indicates the very early understanding that what had happened to Jesus was what was expected for the end of history. The same corollary follows from Paul's description of Jesus' resurrection as 'the first fruits' of the resurrection of 'all' (I Cor. 15.20–23). The imagery is that of the harvest – the 'first fruits' being the first sheaf which was reserved for God. The point is that there would be no gap between cutting the first sheaf and reaping the rest of the harvest. The first fruit was simply the beginning of the harvest. So the description of Jesus' resurrection as the 'first fruit' of the general resurrection could only have been coined by those who thought that with the resurrection of Jesus the final events of history had begun. The same belief is almost certainly mirrored in the otherwise puzzling account of the dead coming out of the tombs and being seen in Jerusalem after Jesus' resurrection (Matt. 27.52–53).

The oddness and unexpectedness of the first Christian belief that God had raised Jesus from the dead should not be discounted. A belief that God had vindicated Jesus or exalted him to heaven after death would have been more understandable. But that they should conclude from these 'sightings' (and from the empty tomb) that God had actually begun the resurrection of the dead is without any real precedent. There must have been something about these first encounters (visionary or otherwise) which pushed them to what was an extraordinary conclusion in the context of that time. A careful jury would have to ask why the first Christians drew such an unusual conclusion. In the light of the considerations outlined above, the answer would be quite proper: A unique explanation for a unique event.

But What do We Mean by 'Resurrection'?

Our task is not quite finished. For thus far we have simply used the key term given us by our sources – 'resurrection'. The empty tomb led to the conclusion, 'God has raised Jesus from the dead'. The 'sightings' were understood as appearances of Jesus as 'raised' by God on the third day after his crucifixion. But what do we mean by 'resurrection'? What actually happened on that third day? What is it that this word which comes now so easily to a Christian's lips describes?

Answer: We don't know! According to our data, no one actually witnessed 'the resurrection'. We cannot even be sure that 'it' could be witnessed. At best a disappearance, or, I suppose, 'dematerialization' of the corpse was as much as would be visible to the eye. 'Resurrection' is itself not part of our data. It is an *inference* drawn from our primary data – empty tomb and appearances. Whether the inference came from heavenly information (as represented, for example, in Matt. 28.6), or as a direct deduction from the events themselves, makes no difference. 'Resurrection' is a deduction not a datum.

More important, when we add the word 'body' to the word 'resurrection' (resurrection body) we have to take note of the fact that the New Testament writers present different conceptions of what a 'resurrection body' is. In Luke's account Jesus' resurrection body is very 'physical': Jesus himself says, 'Handle me and see; for a spirit has not flesh and bones as you see that I have' (Luke 24.39). Paul however makes a clear distinction between the body of this life (= 'physical or natural body') and the resurrection body (= 'spiritual body') (I Cor. 15.42–46). And he concludes his discussion on the point with the ringing declaration: 'I tell you this, brethren: flesh and blood cannot inherit the kingdom of God . . .' (I Cor. 15.50). What Luke affirms (Jesus' resurrection body was flesh and bones) Paul denies (the resurrection body is *not* composed of flesh and blood)!

In view of popular misunderstanding among Christians on this issue the point needs to be clarified and stated with some precision. In I Corinthians Paul seems to have been writing for Greeks who found the idea of the resurrection of this body impossible to imagine (I Cor. 15.12, 35; cf. Acts 17.32). Hence the two most important features of this part of his argument in I Cor. 15. On the one hand he insists on the resurrection of the *body*. But at the same time he makes his distinction between *this* body and the resurrection (= spiritual) body. Paul believed in the resurrection of the *body*, but not the resurrection of *this* body. Properly speaking, then, Paul believed in a 'spiritual' resurrection; 'spiritual' is *his* word. There will be continuity between the person that was and the person that will be. But there will also be difference. Paul himself uses the analogy of the relation between the body of the seed and the body of the plant (I Cor. 15.36–38) – an analogy of continuity, but also of difference between different bodies, between physical body and spiritual body ('You foolish man! . . . What you sow is not the body which is to be . . .'). The flexibility which Paul shows in his conception of the resurrection is a warning to us against thinking that there was a hard and fast, or single, uniform understanding of the resurrection in the beginning.

On the other hand, this recognition of a degree of ambiguity in the concept 'resurrection' should not be made an excuse to empty it of all real content. There is no justification for reducing the meaning of 'the resurrection of Jesus' to something like, 'the continuing significance of Jesus', or 'the disciples' realization that Jesus' message could not die'. By 'resurrection' they clearly meant that something had happened to *Jesus* himself. God had raised *him*, not merely reassured *them*. He was alive again, made alive again with the life which is the climax of God's purpose for humankind, not merely retrieved from the jaws of death but conqueror over death, 'exalted to God's right hand'. It was this glowing conviction which lay at the heart of the chain reaction which began Christianity.

At the same time, it needs to be repeated that any attempt to achieve greater clarity or precision in describing this core of the Christian faith is bound to become increasingly impossible. No event of the past is recoverable, as we noted at the beginning. But an event which was never witnessed by human eye and which by definition breaks through the bounds of history, is an event which goes beyond the capacity of historical description. To that extent at least the concept 'resurrection' can properly be called a 'metaphor' or 'symbol', since it describes something we can only partially and inadequately grasp, and since those of us this side of death (whose language it is) can have no direct experiential knowledge of what we actually do mean by 'resurrection'.

Conclusions

1. It is almost impossible to dispute that at the historical roots of Christianity lie some visionary experiences of the first Christians, who understood them as appearances of Jesus, raised by God from the dead.

2. It is almost as difficult to deny that the emptiness of Jesus' grave was a contributory fact to this earliest conviction of the first Christians.

3. At the same time, Paul's understanding of the resurrection body as a spiritual body strictly speaking does not require an empty grave. The continuity between the body that was and the body that is to be is not of that one-to-one kind. This is why the fact that some bodies are eaten by sharks or blown to pieces and that almost all bodies return to dust does not weaken in any way the Christian hope of 'the resurrection of the body'. In the terms Paul has given us, Christian belief in resurrection is not properly speaking belief in a *physical*

resurrection. Nor is it properly speaking belief in *immortality* (the true 'me' will never die). The Christian believes rather that death is followed by resurrection more in the sense of *recreation*.

4. We therefore have a strange feature at the heart of this fundamental Christian belief about Jesus. At the *historical* level it is very hard to explain how the belief in Jesus' resurrection arose unless his tomb was empty. At the *theological* level, however, the emptiness of the tomb is not necessary to belief in the resurrection. The fact that *both* statements can be made strengthens both – strengthens the historical force of the one and the theological force of the other. It also means that as Luke and Paul differed in their emphases at this point, so Christians today can have similar differences in emphasis, without thereby calling in question the canonical validity or orthodoxy of each other.

5. The Christian interpretation of the basic data (empty tomb and appearances) as 'God raised Jesus from the dead' is a surprising fact for which alternative interpretations of the data fail to provide a more satisfactory explanation.

Has New Testament scholarship made belief in the resurrection of Jesus more difficult? Once again the answer has to be, Yes and No. Yes – but only for those who insist on trying to define 'the resurrection of Jesus' in over-precise terms, or who take the emphasis of one New Testament writer and ignore or play down the emphasis of another. No – for scholarship has clarified *what* the first Christians believed and *why*. Scholarship forces us to recognize that 'the resurrection of Jesus' is an attempt to say something which goes beyond human description. But it also helps us to recognize that there must have been powerful and compelling factors which resulted in the first Christian confession, 'God has raised Jesus from the dead'!

Note on Professor Koester's View

In the first half of the third programme in the series *Jesus: the Evidence*, Professor H. Koester of Harvard University put forward a view which must have been surprising, even astonishing, to many, not excluding many New Testament scholars. His argument was (1) that the first Christians must have followed the normal practice of worshipping at the tomb of Jesus; (2) that the Christians who had abandoned Jerusalem shortly before the outbreak of the Jewish revolt in AD 66 decided to explain the lack of worship at the tomb by saying the tomb was empty; and (3) that as the Gospels were written down years later, the story quickly began to be used to suggest that the tomb had *always* been empty.

(1) The assumption that Christians worshipped at the tomb of Jesus is not supported by any direct evidence whatsoever. Given the probability that a dead prophet's tomb would have provided a focal point for worship by his continuing disciples, the absence of any allusion to such worship has to be explained, either by the hypothesis of an empty tomb (and therefore the only reason for focussing the memory at the tomb was removed – no allusion, because no worship!), or by arguing that such allusions have been suppressed. In the light of the complementary considerations marshalled above the former must surely be judged the more probable.

(2) and (3) Professor Koester envisages a process of creation and development in the tradition of the empty tomb which started about AD 66 and which must have taken a number of years to reach its present form in Mark 16. But most scholars would say that Mark's Gospel was probably written before AD 70, very likely in Rome, and that Mark was using older tradition in Mark 16 as elsewhere. Professor Koester himself thinks a date shortly after AD 70 for the time of composition of Mark is likely, and locates its place of composition in Antioch or some other city in western Syria. But he also thinks that there are indications elsewhere (John's Gospel and the Gospel of Peter) of an earlier form of the empty tomb narrative (earlier than Mark). However, the suggestion that a story put about by some ex-Jerusalem Christians should have become widely spread and firmly enough established among the Christian congregations at large for it to be 'received tradition' used by Mark and those before him within about three or four years, is a good deal less plausible

than the traditional story that Jesus' tomb was found empty on the
first Easter Sunday morning.

We may simply contrast the conclusion reached by the Jewish
scholar, Geza Vermes, who presumably has fewer axes to grind on
this subject than Christian scholars: 'In the end, when every argument
has been considered and weighed, the only conclusion acceptable to
the historian must be . . . that the women who set out to pay their
last respects to Jesus found to their consternation, not a body, but
an empty tomb' (*Jesus the Jew*, Collins 1973, p. 41).

4 Earliest Christianity: One Church or Warring Sects?

A fourth topic probed by the series *Jesus: the Evidence* was the emergence of the Christian church as such. Here too disturbing issues were raised for many Christians – not least by the assertion that 'right from the beginning Christianity was split between different factions vying for supremacy'. Indeed, one might say that an underlying purpose of the series was to pose the challenging question: Have ordinary Christians been told the whole truth? Have the findings of scholars been kept from the ordinary believer? And in this case, if anything the more serious question: Have recent discoveries shed new light on the beginnings of Christianity which require us to revise our picture of what Christianity was like in the first decades of its existence? Those who saw the television programmes will recall how the series began and ended, with the limited-budget portrayal of early Christian theologians coming to blows at the fourth-century Council of Nicaea on issues of doctrinal disagreement. And viewers were shown more than once the film sequences of documents being uncovered from Egyptian cave and sand, with the unspoken inference ready to hand that these documents contained new and disturbing revelations for the faithful about the true story of Christianity's beginnings.

Here too the same question poses itself: Has biblical scholarship and the scholarship of early church historians effectively undermined the beliefs about Christianity's origins still cherished in most Christian churches? And here once again, I'm afraid, the question has to be answered with a Yes *and* No. Yes! – for scholarship certainly has been fairly effective in undermining what one scholar has called 'the myth of Christian beginnings'. There are some beliefs about the emergence of the Christian church which should be undermined – no matter how cherished they may be! But if the question has in view more fundamental beliefs about the character of Christianity as a whole, then the answer is No! And if the scholarship in view is the very lop-sided presentation of the third programme of *Jesus: the Evidence*, the answer is certainly No!

The Myth of Christian Beginnings

There is a popular view of Christian origins which fascinates and deeply influences many Christians. It is the view that the church of the beginning period was the church as it should be, that the first expression of Christianity was the finest expression of Christianity. This is not simply a case of idealizing the past, of harking back to a long departed Golden Age. Apart from anything else, the Golden Age of a nation or a movement does not usually coincide with the first emergence of that nation or movement. Nor is it simply a case of glorifying founder members, a romantic fascination with beginnings as such, producing a larger than life portrayal of how the church began.

The myth of the perfect original form of Christianity emerges more from the centrality of Christ to Christianity. The assumption is that to have been with Jesus when he was on earth must be the most desirable relationship with Jesus possible for the disciple of Jesus. Next best would be to have heard directly from and enjoyed the company of those who were themselves with Jesus, his first disciples. The almost inevitable result is an idealization of *the apostolic age*. The age of the apostles as the age of power, when the word of God was preached with astounding effectiveness, attested by signs and wonders from God. The age of the apostles as the age of purity, when the gospel was unadulterated, before false teaching and heresy appeared. The age of the apostles as the age of perfection, when the church was undivided, united by a common spirit and love. One church, one faith, one baptism.

On this view it becomes significant that the following epoch of Christianity should be called the sub-apostolic age. For not only is it the epoch which *followed* the death of the apostles. But the very prefix *sub-* (subapostolic) implies something on a *lower* level, an *inferior* stage of Christian history. Subconsciously evoked is the parallel with the opening chapters of Genesis – paradise followed by fall. The age of Jésus and his apostles seen as the new creation's period of paradise, the period following, by implication, a fallen state.

To be fair, this view of Christian beginnings is given some credibility within the New Testament itself. Consider the words of Paul in taking leave of the elders of Ephesus as we have them in Acts 20.29–30:

> I know that after my departure fierce wolves will come in among you, not sparing the flock; and from among your own selves will arise men speaking perverse things, to draw away the disciples after them.

Similarly the forebodings of I Timothy 4.1–3:

> Now the Spirit expressly says that in later times some will depart from

the faith by giving heed to deceitful spirits and doctrines of demons, through the pretensions of liars whose consciences are seared, who forbid marriage and enjoin abstinence from foods which God created to be received with thanksgiving by those who believe and know the truth.

In both passages the picture is of a period following the death of the apostles when ravening wolves would begin to break in from outside and to worry the flock with false teaching, an age when many in the church would abandon their first love and decline into unbelief.

This view was powerfully reinforced in the patristic period when the fight against heresy resulted in an increasing idealization of Christian beginnings. During the apostolic age the church had remained a virgin, pure and uncorrupted. But since then false teachers had tried to defile it with godless error. The apostolic age had been the age of truth. Error was innovation. In the words of Tertullian, one of the most forceful of the earliest Fathers:

Were Christians found before Christ? Or heresy before true doctrine? But in everything truth precedes its counterfeit. It would be absurd to regard heresy as the prior doctrine since it is prophesied that heresy should arise (*Prescription against Heretics* 29).

In the past hundred years or so such views have continued to exercise a powerful influence in both the scholarly and the popular perception of how Christianity began. A good example is the great Protestant scholar Adolf von Harnack, whose lectures on the essence of Christianity at the beginning of the twentieth century were widely influential. For Harnack the ideal time was restricted more or less to Jesus' own ministry; and the ideal form of Christianity was the teaching of Jesus. The simple, pure message of Jesus about the father-hood of God and the brotherhood of man had unfortunately soon been corrupted by the process of translating and expanding it into the categories of Greek philosophy – a process which began already with Paul! More prominent today is the desire among many Christians to recapture the drive and zeal of the first Christians. 'Back to the Bible!' is still a powerful slogan. 'Back to New Testament Christ-ianity!' is the motivation which inspires many a Christian group to try to recreate and relive the church pattern of the apostolic age.

In all this there is a subtle tendency to treat the period of Christian beginnings as qualitatively different, a time separate and distinct from what followed – a kind of timeless age, not subject to the same forces of change and decay which the forms and organizations of this world know all too well. Hence indeed the preference for such phrases as 'the apostolic age', 'New Testament Christianity': to speak of 'first-

century Christianity' is too rudely this-worldly; it locates earliest
Christianity too firmly within the ebb and flow of ordinary history.

The diversity of denominations

With the Reformation, of course, *different* church patterns emerged
in Western Christianity. Yet, somewhat surprisingly, this new situation made little difference to the still universal view of Christian
beginnings. The different denominations continued to hold the same
belief about the character of earliest Christianity. They simply applied
the universal thesis to their own denomination, each maintaining that
they (their denomination, their form of the church) were most nearly
in accord with the original pattern.

The trouble was that each denomination saw its *own* pattern within
the New Testament. They treated the New Testament as a kind of
mirror, which, not surprisingly, reflected their own convictions and
prejudices – Catholic, Lutheran and Reformed (Presbyterian),
Anglican, Baptist and Independent. That would not have been so
serious – except that in order to maintain the belief that *they* were
right, they had to maintain also that the *others* were *wrong*. They
were the true heirs of the apostolic church; the others were the false
teachers with their deluded flocks. So wrong were they that they had
to be denounced and where possible rooted out.

Historical scholarship has helped us to see that such views are *all*
an oversimplification. The reason why each can see its own image in
the mirror of the New Testament is simple – because *all* are there.
All the different church orders current today can be validated from
the New Testament. If episcopacy, presbyterianism, congregational
and baptist ecclesiologies can each be justified individually, then *all*
can be justified. The diversity of patterns of church organization and
ministry had already been recognized more than a hundred years ago
by one of Durham's greatest scholar-bishops, J. B. Lightfoot, in his
magisterial treatment of 'The Christian Ministry' (1868).

The Diversity of Christianity in the First Century

At first this recognition of diverse forms of Christianity within the
New Testament could be simply countered by the argument that the
whole style of church order was not yet clearly developed in the New
Testament. At the time the New Testament documents were written,
Christian church order was only at an embryonic stage. The full or
proper church order emerged only later. In this way the range of
ecclesiologies within the New Testament itself could be made less
threatening.

But then it came to be more clearly realized that what the New Testament shows is not just undeveloped diversity but genuine diversity. The diversity of first-century Christianity could not be discounted as simply unthought out expressions of faith, unworked out forms of corporate life. There were real and important differences between the Christians of the founding period in their understanding of what Christianity was and of how it should be expressed. And not just on peripheral or secondary matters – on some central matters as well. And not just diversity and difference, but disagreement and controversy, sometimes on very important issues.

Consider the following passages from Paul's letters – bearing in mind that Paul's are the only New Testament documents which we can be sure come from the first generation of Christianity, the apostolic age *par excellence*!

First of all from Galatians 1.6–9:

> I am astonished that you are so quickly deserting him who called you in the grace of Christ and turning to a different gospel – not that there is another gospel, but there are some who trouble you and want to pervert the gospel of Christ. But even if we, or an angel from heaven, should preach to you a gospel contrary to (or at variance with) that which we preached to you, let him be accursed. As we have said before, so now I say again, If any one is preaching to you a gospel contrary to that which you received, let him be accursed.

At first, because the words are so familiar, we may assume that Paul is attacking enemies of Christianity – presumably Jews who held the same attitude to Christianity which Paul himself had maintained before his conversion. But with a little more thought we quickly realize that Paul is actually attacking fellow Christians, or at least people who made the same claim to belief in Christ as Paul did himself. Like Paul they understood their message as 'gospel'; it is Paul who calls it 'a different gospel'. Like Paul they thought of their message as 'the gospel of Christ'; Paul accepts that title to the extent that he sees their message as a perversion of that gospel, but not an outright denial of or contradiction to it. The message was obviously attractive to the Galatians – they too cannot have seen it as outright opposition to what they had heard from Paul; Paul has to play down its attractiveness – 'even if we, or an angel from heaven . . .'. What is in view was evidently a subtle variation on Paul's own gospel, rather than something self-evidently false. Paul's response to this different understanding of what faith in Christ involved is abrupt: 'Let him be accursed'! The sentiment, we might note, is a good deal closer to the polemics of the Reformation era than to the gentler language of today's 'conversations'.

In the very next chapter of Galatians Paul returns to the attack. He tells how the Gentile convert, Titus, was a test case in the debate on whether Gentiles needed to be circumcised in order to become Christians. The debate took place in Jerusalem and involved Paul and Barnabas, the Jerusalem leadership (particularly James, Peter and John), and those whom Paul calls 'false brethren'.

> I laid before them (but privately before those who were of repute) the gospel which I preach among the Gentiles, lest somehow I should be running or had run in vain. But even Titus, who was with me, was not compelled to be circumcised, though he was a Greek. But because of false brethren secretly brought in, who slipped in to spy out our freedom which we have in Christ Jesus, that they might bring us into bondage – to them we did not yield submission even for a moment, that the truth of the gospel might be preserved for you. And from those who were reputed to be something (what they were makes no difference to me; God shows no partiality) – those, I say, who were of repute added nothing to me (Gal. 2.2–6).

Here again it would be too easy to dismiss 'the false brethren' as only 'pretend Christians', fifth columnists of an alien faith. But once again that would be unfair to 'the false brethren'. Since they were fully involved in the debate within the Jerusalem church about the requirements laid on Gentile converts to faith in Christ, they must have been regarded as acceptable to or in good standing with the Jerusalem leadership – on the conservative wing of the Judaean church, no doubt, but members of the congregations who named the name of Jesus none the less. It is Paul who calls their Christian profession in some question, so certain was he that their understanding of what being a Christian involved was too narrow and constrictive of Christian freedom.

We might just note also in passing that his attitude to the Jerusalem leadership itself shows a vigorous independence and unwillingness to opt for easy compromise. He calls them 'those who were reputed to be something' – a distancing phrase which acknowledges that they were held in high reputation – but not necessarily by him! And he adds in parenthesis: 'what they once were makes no difference to me – God shows no favouritism' (2.6 – RSV does not bring out the full force of the parenthesis).

Most striking of all is the fierceness of Paul's language in chapter 5 of the same letter – Gal. 5.1–12. Here Paul urges his readers strongly to resist the temptation to compromise their freedom by accepting what we can now see is best identified as a narrower understanding of Christian faith.

> For freedom Christ has set us free; stand fast therefore, and do not submit again to a yoke of slavery. Now I, Paul, say to you that if you

receive circumcision, Christ will be of no advantage to you. I testify again to every man who receives circumcision that he is bound to keep the whole law. You are severed from Christ, you who would be justified by the law; you have fallen away from grace. For through the Spirit, by faith, we wait for the hope of righteousness. For in Christ Jesus neither circumcision nor uncircumcision is of any avail, but faith working through love. You were running well; who hindered you from obeying the truth? This persuasion is not from him who called you. . . .

And so on – ending with the astonishing outburst:

I wish those who unsettle you would mutilate themselves!

Once again RSV has given us a softer rendering than the Greek calls for. The force of Paul's outburst would be given better if we translated bluntly:

I wish those who unsettle you would castrate themselves!

Or as the Jerusalem Bible neatly puts it:

Tell those who are disturbing you (with calls for your circumcision) I would like to see the knife slip.

Not quite the language of constructive ecumenical dialogue!

Lest it be thought that Paul wrote Galatians on an off-day and that elsewhere he is a paragon of ecumenical openness and understanding, we should just note two other letters where the same sort of passionate denunciation appears – II Corinthians 11. 3–5, 13–15 and Philippians 3.2.

I am afraid that as the serpent deceived Eve by his cunning, your thoughts will be led astray from a sincere and pure devotion to Christ. For if someone comes and preaches another Jesus than the one we preached, or if you receive a different spirit from the one you received, or if you accept a different gospel from the one you accepted, you submit to it readily enough (II Cor. 11.3–4).

The language and intent is very similar to that of the first Galatians passage. And the same deduction can be made. Those attacked by Paul would clearly not regard themselves as opponents of faith in Christ. They preached Jesus. Reception of the Spirit was as important for them as for Paul. Theirs too was a gospel offer. Paul here is attacking Christian evangelists who evidently understood Christianity somewhat differently from Paul – but Christian evangelists none the less.

More striking still is the passage which follows:

I think that I am not in the least inferior to these superlative apostles . . . For such men are false apostles, deceitful workmen, disguising themselves as apostles of Christ. And no wonder, for even

Satan disguises himself as an angel of light. So it is not strange if his servants also disguise themselves as servants of righteousness. Their end will correspond to their deeds (II Cor. 11.5, 13–15).

Paul here is attacking not simply Christian evangelists, but Christian apostles! Clearly they called themselves 'apostles of Christ'. Paul calls them 'superlative apostles'. The phrase signifies both that they were very highly regarded as apostles, and that Paul's view of their status was not a little jaundiced. But worse is to follow! They are 'false apostles', 'servants of Satan'! Clearly there is a rift here of some magnitude between two bands of Christian missionaries, indeed we may say between two branches of Christianity, or even between two kinds of Christianity. And the differences between them are not minor squabbles but focus on central questions of what Christianity is and how it should be lived out.

The final passage worth noting in Paul is Philippians 3.2 – 'Look out for the dogs, look out for the evil workers, look out for those who mutilate the flesh'. Again the target is the same – fellow Jews who insisted that Gentile conversion to Christ must be marked by circumcision. From the parallel with the passages in II Corinthians and Galatians we may fairly conclude that they were not simply fellow Jews, but fellow Jewish Christians. And again the language is fierce – 'dogs' – an insult presumably as offensive then as the modern American slang, 'son of a bitch'! Here too we need to shake ourselves and remember that Paul is probably speaking once again of Christians! Hardly the sort of language to inspire mutual respect and confidence.

Unfortunately we have no writings from Paul's Jewish Christian opponents preserved for us – not in the New Testament anyway. That, however, should not be taken as an excuse to dismiss these opponents simply as unreformed Jews or as heretics before the concept of heresy had been formulated. The fact is that the viewpoint which Paul resists so fiercely can be identified in greater or less degree with the form of Christianity which held sway in the mother church of Christianity – Jerusalem itself. The book of Acts represents their position very vividly. When Paul returns from his missionary endeavours for the last time to Jerusalem, he is met by James (the brother of Jesus) and the elders, who at once tell him:

> You see, brother, how many thousands there are among the Jews of those who have believed; they are all zealous for the law, and they have been told about you that you teach all the Jews who are among the Gentiles to forsake Moses, telling them not to circumcise their children or observe the customs (Acts 21.20–21).

That more extreme expression of Jewish Christian faith ('all zealous for the law') is, as I have said, not represented within the New Testament documents themselves. But there are more modified versions of it. They come some way towards Paul, but still preserve the emphases of a somewhat different understanding of what it means to become and to be a Christian. The most striking example is James 2.18–24:

> Some one will say, 'You have faith and I have works'. Show me your faith apart from your works, and I by my works will show you my faith. You believe that God is one; you do well. Even the demons believe – and shudder. Do you want to be shown, you foolish fellow, that faith apart from works is barren? Was not Abraham our father justified by works, when he offered his son Isaac upon the altar? You see that faith was active along with his works, and faith was completed by works, and the scripture was fulfilled which says, 'Abraham believed God, and it was reckoned to him as righteousness' [Gen. 15.6]; and he was called the friend of God. You see that a man is justified by works and not by faith alone.

The point here is that the slogan 'justified by faith alone' is almost certainly a Pauline slogan, or at least one derived immediately from Paul's emphasis on the sole sufficiency of faith (as in Rom. 3.28). Indeed, it almost seems as though James has in view Paul's own line of argument in that part of his letter to the Romans. For at the end of Romans 3 Paul uses the same Jewish creed that 'God is one' to advance his *own* argument that God justifies *all* by *faith*. And then, just like James, he immediately goes on in chapter 4 to expound Genesis 15.6 as proving that God justified Abraham by faith and *not* by works. The parallel is so close that we may be pardoned for wondering whether James is not deliberately trying to refute or at least correct Paul's own argument as developed in Romans 3 and 4. At all events, the 'foolish fellow' whom James addresses must have been using an argument very much like Paul's. And even if James does not allude directly to Romans 3–4, it cannot be denied that James' exposition of Genesis 15.6 reads that Old Testament text in a way which is at some odds with Paul's exposition of the same text in Romans 4. The attitude of the letter of James in fact comes close to that expressed in the description of the Jerusalem Christians cited above (p. 86): unlike Paul, James regards the law as 'perfect', 'the law of liberty' (James 1.25). The attribution of the letter to James, the principal leader of the Jerusalem church, from where much hostility towards Paul emerged, is therefore not altogether surprising.

Two Forms of Earliest Christianity

It thus becomes clear that what we have already in the first generation of Christianity is two forms of Christianity. From the passages quoted above and various other indications drawn from both inside and beyond the New Testament, we can build up a clearer picture of these two types – or should we say, branches or even denominations of Christianity? On the one hand, what is most fairly, if still misleadingly, called 'Jewish Christianity'. On the other, what even less adequately can be called 'Gentile Christianity'.

Jewish Christianity

This was the earliest form of Christianity – the form of Christianity which first emerged in Jerusalem and Palestine, and which retained its chief strength there, being undoubtedly the strongest form of Christianity in the Jewish heartland. These (Jewish) Christians felt it important to stress the continuity of the new movement with Judaism – the child (Christianity) taking after its parent. They saw the new movement *not* as a separate religion, but simply what the scholars sometimes call 'eschatological Judaism' – that is, the Judaism of the new age, the Judaism intended by God at the climax of history, but still essentially Judaism. For them Jesus was nothing if he was not the Messiah, the Messiah of Jewish expectation. For them membership of the people of God was still necessary to salvation – and that meant the people of Israel, the Jews. Outside the covenant God had made with his people Israel there could be no salvation.

It followed inevitably for the Jewish Christian that the law was still central to God's purpose of salvation. The law had been given to the covenant people as their badge of belonging and to define their responsibility as members of the covenant people. Obedience to the law was the mark of membership of the people of God. Therefore circumcision was still essential. How could it be otherwise when God had specified so clearly that circumcision was a 'sign of the covenant', as eternal an obligation as the covenant itself? The ruling of scripture was unequivocal: No circumcision, no covenant! 'Any uncircumcised male who is not circumcised in the flesh of his foreskin shall be cut off from his people: he has broken my covenant' (Gen. 17.9–14).

For the same reason other regulations regarded as central to the law of the covenant could not be disregarded and continued to determine (Jewish) Christian life-style and conduct – particularly observance of the sabbath and of the dietary laws (such as we have in Leviticus 11). As we saw above, the chief focus of dispute for Paul was circumcision. But these other elements of the controversy between Jewish and

Gentile Christianity are echoed in such passages as Romans 14.2,5
and Gal. 4.10. In particular, it was disagreement over food laws which
evidently caused the split in the Christian church in Antioch, which
Paul describes in Galatians 2.11–15.

We can also deduce that the pattern of church order which emerged
in Jerusalem was much more closely based on the synagogue model
than we find in Paul – church leader (James) and elders (as in Acts
21.18), in contrast to the more charismatic pattern of prophets and
teachers which we find in the churches most closely associated with
the Gentile mission (as in Acts 13.1–2 and I Cor. 12.28). But it would
take too long to develop the point here.

Gentile Christianity

This was the type of Christianity which emerged when the new
faith in Jesus the Christ began to move out beyond Palestine and
beyond Judaism itself. According to the Acts of the Apostles, this
breakthrough took place in Syrian Antioch (the third largest city of
the Roman Empire). There 'the Hellenists' (Acts 6.1), who had been
identified with Stephen and who were probably the chief targets of
the persecution which followed Stephen's death (Acts 7.57–8.4), first
preached to Greeks (= Gentiles) (Acts 11.20). There it would appear
that increasing numbers of Gentile converts resulted in a form of
Christianity which sat loose to the law, or at least too loose for many
Jerusalem believers (Gal. 2.11–15). And from there Paul went forth
as a missionary (Acts 13.1–3) and began a sequence of missionary
operations which demonstrated his claim to be 'apostle to the
Gentiles'.

'Gentile Christianity', in other words, is a way of describing the
form of Christianity which emerged particularly in the churches
founded by Paul. If Paul himself is any guide, these congregations
still maintained strongly that they stood in continuity with Judaism.
That is why the title 'Gentile Christianity' is less than adequate: many
Jews, including Paul, belonged to this growing stream of Christianity;
just as, no doubt, there were at least some Gentiles who 'judaized'
all the way to what we are here calling 'Jewish Christianity'.

The difference was that the Jewish heritage claimed by Gentile
Christianity was a Judaism transformed, a Judaism wholly open to
Gentiles on equal terms with Jews. Membership of the covenant
people of God was now understood to be determined wholly by faith
– as Paul taught his converts so forcefully in arguments summed up
in Galatians 3 and Romans 4. Circumcision was no longer necessary
– a major departure from such a clearly worded commandment of
scripture (Gen. 17). Membership of the people of God was no longer

to be thought of as dependent on keeping food laws and sabbath. What began on the basis of faith should continue on that basis.

The free-er life-style of Gentile Christianity (free-er in respect of the Jewish law) was probably mirrored in the free-er forms of worship and ministry which Paul seems to encourage in such chapters as Romans 12 and I Corinthians 12.

No doubt the patterns grouped under these two headings (Jewish Christianity and Gentile Christianity) were a good deal more complex and overlapped to a greater extent than we have time to explore here. No doubt too there were many factors involved – theological, social, cultural, and so on. And for all their differences, we must always recall that they were part of the same movement (Christianity), held together by their common faith in Jesus as God's Messiah and Son, raised by God from the dead as the beginning of the new age, and probably also by the breadth of vision and sympathy of Peter in particular. But it is clear, nevertheless, that in the beginning there were at least two major divergent patterns of Christianity, and that the diversity was more than simply a difference of emphasis or a difference in detail. However uncomfortable the historical conclusion may be, we can hardly avoid speaking of different forms or styles or types of first-century Christiantiy – that is, of apostolic Christianity.

The spectrum of first-century Christianity

The diverse patterns of first-century Christianity can be illustrated diagramatically. Once again it should be clearly understood that the diagram opposite is inadequate: for better effect it would need to be three-dimensional; and both dating and relative positioning of some of the New Testament documents are very tentative. The diagram is illustrative rather than definitive. But for all its roughness, at least the diagram helps to bring out the point that first-century Christianity did not consist of clearly distinct groups. In its earliest years, Christianity quickly became more like a spectrum (a three-dimensional spectrum, remember), with quite considerable divergence and disagreement between the ends.

The diagram needs little interpretation. As we now know more clearly, first-century Judaism itself was far from being a monolithic or homogeneous faith. It too was more of a spectrum. The common ground centred on the conviction that the one God had chosen Israel as his people and had given the law to direct their life. But that central conviction was understood and lived out in a range of different ways and degrees by the mass of the people and by the various special

First century	J	U	D	A	I	S	M

30   J E S U S

                                    First Christians

                     Hellenists   Jerusalem
                                                   Christians

                     P a u l   Opponents
60   of Paul

                           Mark

                     Hebrews   I Peter   James

                     Luke-Acts   Matthew

90   J o h n   Pastorals

Second century	Gnostic Christianity		Catholic Christianity	Jewish Christianity		Rabbinic Judaism

(Diagonal labels at right: Pharisees, Essenes, Zealots)

interest groups within Judaism – Sadducees, Pharisees, Essenes, and later, Zealots.

Within this spectrum of first-century Judaism, the impact of Jesus gave rise to two main emphases, as outlined above. (1) A version of reformed or eschatological Judaism, which still thought of itself in Jewish terms, as defined in terms of the Jewish people, as marked out by the traditional boundaries of Judaism as well as the newer boundary of baptism in the name of Jesus. On the diagram this side of Christianity is denoted particularly by the labels 'Jerusalem Christians' and 'Opponents of Paul'. (2) A movement to draw in Gentiles more and more, and solely on the basis of faith in Jesus – that is, of course, on the basis of faith in Jesus as the agent of the same one God and raised by him from death. But the particular emphasis on the sole sufficiency of faith in God alone (without 'works of the law') involved a decisive change in the older understanding of what it meant to be the people of God. On the diagram this developing and different form of Christianity is denoted by the labels 'Hellenists' and 'Paul'.

On the spectrum of first-century or apostolic Christianity, the ends of the spectrum merged into the wider spectrum of first-century religion in the eastern end of the Mediterranean. Christianity seen as reformed or eschatological Judaism (1) was simply part of the larger spectrum of first-century Judaism and overlapped with other interest groups on that spectrum. That is why on the diagram the opponents of Paul are shown as overlapping with the Pharisees. According to Acts 15.5 'some believers belonged to the party of the Pharisees'. Another indication of the overlap is the difficulty of knowing whether the phrase 'those of the circumcision' ('the circumcision party' in RSV – Acts 11.2 and Gal. 2.12) means Jews or more particularly Jewish Christians.

At the other end of the spectrum of first-century Christianity, the developing Gentile Christianity (2) began to merge into the larger religiosity of the wider Greek world. This wider religiosity was typically syncretistic. That is to say, it willingly saw different national religions as simply part of a single more universal religion. And frequently different elements from different religious systems were combined to form new hybrids. Within this wider pattern of religion the new Christian movement would seem to many to be simply one further variation on a common theme and to provide opportunity for further permutations and combinations. We can see something of this happening in the churches at Corinth (Greece) and Colossae (Asia Minor). For example, a number of the Corinthian Christians obviously made much of 'wisdom' and 'knowledge' (I Cor. 1–3, 8) and seem to have reacted against the Christian claim that the body would be raised (I Cor. 15). Such ideas and attitudes were characteristic of the wider Greek religious traditions. And at Colossae the mixture included 'philosophy . . . according to the elemental spirits of the universe', 'questions of food and drink', observance of new moon and sabbath (notice the Jewish element), 'worship of angels' and visions (Col. 2.8–18).

Of course the New Testament writers themselves do not regard this merging of the Christian spectrum into other forms of religion as desirable. Paul, as we have seen, warns fiercely against confusing Christianity with the older understanding of Judaism. And he, and subsequently other New Testament writers, warns no less strenuously against those who were in danger of losing sight of Christianity's distinctiveness. Nevertheless, the uncomfortable fact remains that the historical reality of the earliest Christian churches was quite different from the ideal so often projected back upon 'the apostolic church' by later Christians.

To that extent, at any rate, *Jesus: the Evidence* was justified in its portrayal of Christian beginnings. But the claims made in that series were more far reaching, and since they take us beyond the limits of the New Testament and of the first century, we must pursue our own analysis a little further (still with reference to the diagram on the previous page).

Earliest Christianity in the Second and Subsequent Generations

The second generation of Christianity showed no real narrowing of the spectrum thus far described, no real lessening of the diversity. For the evidence here we must refer to the New Testament documents written between about AD 65 and 100 and to the Christianity they represent. On a two-dimensional diagram, of course, it is not possible to represent the true interrelationships of these second generation writings of first-century Christianity. Certainly they continue to cohere in their common faith in Christ as God's man and their Lord – with all that that involves for other beliefs and for worship. But it would be unfair to them not to recognize their distinct emphases within that common faith and life.

The diagram attempts to represent something of this, though in a necessarily incomplete way: Mark, probably the earliest of the Gospels, close to Paul in his emphasis on Christ's passion; I Peter too with some characteristic Pauline emphases; Hebrews with its own very distinctive way of speaking of Jesus using both Jewish categories and the categories of Greek philosophy. Towards the other end of the spectrum, James, as we have already suggested; with Matthew not so far from Paul in emphasis, but certainly the most characteristically Jewish of the Gospels; and Luke-Acts probably providing something of a bridge between Paul and the rest of Christianity, focussing on Paul alone as the hero of the second half of Acts, but presenting him as much more amenable to the emphases stemming from Jerusalem than his own letters would suggest.

Towards the end of the first century we should probably locate the New Testament writings which became most influential in determining the subsequent doctrine of Christ and in setting the pattern for the future structure of the church catholic. I refer, on the one hand, to John's Gospel with its high (and as we have seen, developed) view of Christ, which also shows knowledge of the wider religious speculation of the time. And, on the other, to the Pastoral Epistles (I and II Timothy and Titus), which give clear evidence of a more institutionalized pattern of church order already becoming established (bishops, elders, deacons).

As we move into the second century the spectrum begins to assume a more regular pattern, with the options more clearly defined, and the opposite ends of the spectrum beginning to form more clearly distinct and different kinds of Christianity.

Catholic Christianity

The strongest currents in the different forms of first-century Christianity flowed into Catholic Christianity, which thus became the mainstream of the Christian tradition and church, and which two centuries
later became the established religion of the Roman Empire. Its
distinctive characteristics were formed by the emergence of a clear-
cut ecclesiastical organization and a firmly defined 'rule of faith'.

In the second century episcopacy steadily gained ground within
Catholic Christianity, as the most desirable and necessary pattern of
church order – the bishop as the focus of unity and the bulwark
against false teaching. Hand in hand with this came the re-emergence
of the distinction between clergy and laity, priest and people – an
Old Testament distinction which had been left behind in the New
Testament period, but which now once again began to become part
of the self-understanding of Catholic Christianity. By the same
process the sacraments became increasingly prominent in the Catholic
understanding of salvation, and more and more exclusively the means
of grace.

The 'rule of faith' emerged as a related development. With the
passage of the second century there came a growing sense of need
for Catholic Christians to distinguish the true faith from its corrupt
forms and unacceptable substitutes. There were too many others
laying claim to be heirs of the heritage left by Jesus and the apostles.
The true heirs had to defend their inheritance. So for the first time
we can begin to speak of a clear sense of Christian 'orthodoxy', as a
firmly defined faith distinguished from competing definitions, which
could in turn be dismissed as 'heresy'.

A fundamental part of this emerging self-definition of Catholic
Christianity was the recognition of the need to define which writings
from the first generations were to be regarded as authoritative and
to be marked off from others. And thus the documents which we call
the New Testament began to be set apart from other writings, which
also claimed the inspiration of the Spirit, to function as a 'canon',
that is, as a yardstick of orthodoxy, a criterion of the catholic faith.

In this last development there was a certain element of irony. For
the fact is that the range of Christianity encompassed within the New
Testament documents is actually broader than the Catholic Christianity which recognized their canonicity. Even though the spectrum
of New Testament Christianity is narrower than the spectrum of
first-century Christianity, there are various elements within the New
Testament spectrum which, if truth be told, fitted rather uncomfort-
ably within the increasingly tight definitions of Catholic Christianity.

I am thinking, for example, of the fact that Jesus himself seems deliberately to have avoided setting up ritual boundaries for his would-be disciples to observe: he practised no baptism, and his table-fellowship was criticized for its openness. Alternatively, consider the 'enthusiastic' features in Acts: for those critical of 'enthusiasm' it is inevitably somewhat perturbing to note that the first Christians seem to have thrived on a diet of visions, experiences of ecstatic inspiration and miracles. Or think again of the very charismatic character of Paul's idea of the body of Christ, of Hebrews' strong denial of a distinct priesthood within the new covenant people of God (distinctions between priesthood and people belonging to the *old* covenant), or of the individualism of John which has reminded many commentators more of the piety to be found in Christian conventions for the deepening of the spiritual life than of the more formal patterns of catholic worship.

In drawing up the canon of the New Testament the early fathers of the church catholic certainly took a major step forward in defining Christianity and in marking it off from all competing or counterfeit forms. But the canon they actually drew up defines a Christianity which is in fact larger than their own perception of Christianity!

If Catholic Christianity was the mainstream to emerge from the first century, we should also note that there were two other quite strong streams which emerged on either side, as it were, of the mainstream – different forms of Jewish Christiantiy, and a variety of movements which fall under the heading of 'Gnostic Christianity'.

Jewish Christianity

Israel rebelled against its Roman overlords twice within seventy years – first in the second half of the 60s and again in the early 130s. Both revolts failed – as was almost inevitable (apart from divine intervention), given the disparity between the two opponents. And with their failure, the destruction of the Jerusalem temple and the subjugation of the heartland of Judaism, much of Judaism's earlier diversity either disappeared or faded in significance. The form which survived with greatest strength was the Judaism of the Pharisees. They regrouped and reorganized and began the same process as Catholic Christianity – that of defining their faith more clearly, what was acceptable and unacceptable, their own canon of scripture (what Christians call the Old Testament). This form of Judaism, rabbinic Judaism, in due course became Judaism proper, the trunk from which grew the different branches of Judaism as we know them today.

One of the forms of the earlier more diverse Judaism which the rabbis disowned was Christianity. As Catholic Christianity and rabbinic Judaism each began to define itself with greater precision, so each began to pull away from the other. The two streams from the same headwater flowed in divergent channels. In the widening gap between these two main religious movements were left those groups which had previously been able to thrive in the overlap between Christianity and Judaism – hybrid forms of Jewish Christianity, both Jewish and Christian, but increasingly unacceptable to both.

Some of these Jewish Christian groups could trace a respectable line of descent from the earliest form of Jewish Christianity in Jerusalem. But as, Christianity grew and developed, as the emphases of Paul, of Gentile Christianity and of John became accepted as integral parts of Christianity proper, so these older undeveloped forms of Christianity became increasingly dated and increasingly unacceptable to catholic Christians. For the Jewish Christian of the second and third centuries, Jesus was simply a prophet, James the first sole leader of the Jerusalem church was the great hero, and Paul who had transformed the faith by opening the door so wide to the Gentiles was a renegade and apostate. Such Jewish Christian sects survived for a century or two, but without the vitality of Catholic Christianity or the determined purpose of rabbinic Judaism they slowly withered and died. With them what had been a wing of apostolic Christianity effectively disappeared from the spectrum of Christianity, diminishing that spectrum, and giving free-er rein to some less than desirable anti-Jewish tendencies among the remaining catholic faithful.

Gnostic Christianity

At the other end of the spectrum of first-century Christianity, it will be recalled, came the more mixed or syncretistic forms of Christianity. Again we should simply pause and remind ourselves that a two-dimensional spectrum is inadequate to represent the complexity of the situation, including the way in which each 'end' of the spectrum could and did influence the other. In the second century this larger syncretistic religiosity began to take shape in a number of different religious systems which can be grouped under the general head 'Gnosticism'. When elements of Christian faith were included we can speak of 'Gnostic Christianity'.

The Gnostic movements of the second century were quite varied in particular points of emphasis. But, speaking in generalized terms, they shared a number of basic convictions which in greater or less degree were common to them all. Chief of these were: (1) A sharp dualism between spirit and matter, and between the upper world and the lower world. Spirit alone was of heaven and good. Matter was of the lower world, corrupted and evil. (2) The soul was a divine spark in man, a piece of heavenly spirit fallen to earth and imprisoned within the material body, enclosed and stifled by the despised 'mud' of the flesh. (3) Salvation consisted in recalling the soul to its true nature by providing it with knowledge (Greek, *'gnosis'*) of its true home and with instructions on the way back to the upper world. In Christian Gnosticism the Christian element added to the syncretistic mix was (4) belief in Christ as a heavenly being who came down to earth to give the vital *gnosis* to the lost souls. As a wholly spiritual being, Christ only entered the man Jesus or appeared to be human, but was really unchangingly divine and never truly united with human flesh.

Up until the beginning of the twentieth century, Gnosticism was thought to be an offshoot of Christianity, just another set of Christian heresies. But since then it has become widely recognized in scholarly circles that many of the basic elements of the Gnostic systems were already current at the time of Jesus and the first Christians, if not even earlier. Much of the twentieth-century scholarly debate about Christian beginnings has thus focussed on the question of whether Gnosticism was already in full flower before Christianity and whether Christianity borrowed its ideas about Christ as heavenly redeemer from Gnosticism, rather than the other way round. The largest consensus has now reverted to a modified version of the older view: gnostic ideas were part of the wider syncretistic religiosity of the first century; but full-blown Gnosticism appeared only in the second century. And to the extent that the Gnostic systems gave place to a divine redeemer figure they probably did in fact draw this element chiefly from Christianity. Gnostic Christianity as such does not appear until the second century.

At this point, however, *Jesus: the Evidence* sounded a very different note. It presented the thesis that Gnostic Christianity was a third major strand of Christianity, more or less as old as the other two strands (Jewish Christianity and Gentile Christianity), and with equal claim to reflect the true teaching of Jesus as the other strands. In other words, the tensions afflicting first-century Christianity involved not only Jewish and Gentile Christians, but also Gnostic Christians. This was presented not as a thesis proposed by a few scholars, which it is, but as a matter of fact. How these Gnostic churches emerged was not made clear. But at least an explanation had earlier been offered for our lack of knowledge of them before now – namely, the corollary thesis that evidence of and documents from these churches were suppressed and destroyed when Catholic Christianity gained the upper hand. That there is a large measure of truth in this is not to be doubted, although it must have been a remarkably powerful Catholic church which could obliterate so completely all trace of the first-century Gnostic churches.

Not quite all, however, according to *Jesus: the Evidence*. The new thesis of first-century Gnostic churches is put forward on the basis of documents found near the town of Nag Hammadi in Upper Egypt in December 1945. The reconstructed scene of the discovery was replayed more than once in the first and third programmes of *Jesus: the Evidence*. These were the documents mentioned at the beginning of the present chapter, the documents whose uncovering, it was inferred, gave a very different picture of Christian beginnings from what had hitherto been accepted in Christian circles.

But is the inference justified? What *do* these documents tell us about the beginnings of Christianity, or, more precisely, of Gnostic Christianity? Most of the Nag Hammadi documents are indeed strongly Gnostic in character, and so provide an invaluable first-hand insight into Gnosticism in general and Gnostic Christianity in particular, where previously we have had to depend on the polemical accounts of the catholic fathers. But they do not really provide proof of a *first*-century Gnostic Christianity. The documents themselves were all written in the fourth century and go far to confirm the picture of second and third century Gnosticism as we already knew it. And while they do contain evidence of older traditions, Christian and non-Christian, the real argument focusses on the issue of whether the *Gnostic* elements are as old as or older than earliest Christianity. Here, it has to be said, the thesis depends on special pleading – particularly on the argument that an idea which shows no Christian influence must therefore be older than (or as old as) Christianity. A highly dubious argument, and one which has persuaded only a few scholars. The more obvious interpretation of the Nag Hammadi documents is that they are all typically syncretistic: they draw bits and pieces from a wide range of religious influences in the ancient world, including Judaism and Christianity, but including others too. As such they are wholly explainable in terms of what we now know about second- and third-century Gnosticism.

In short, the suggestion that there were Gnostic churches already in the first century is an unnecessary hypothesis. And if *Jesus: the Evidence* was attempting to give a balanced view of how modern historical scholarship now sees the beginnings of Christianity, it failed lamentably at this point. So far as the period covered by the New Testament documents is concerned, we are dealing with a more limited spectrum, where the chief factors making for tension were the Jewish Christianity which looked to James on one side and the Gentile Christianity of which Paul was representative on the other.

Conclusions

1. Earliest Christianity was quite a *diverse* phenomenon. Within the spectrum of apostolic Christianity there was considerable room for different emphases. And not only different emphases, but also some quite serious disagreements. From one point of view this is a depressing conclusion; (to strip away illusions and take off rose-tinted spectacles can have a depressing effect). The Christianity established by the first apostles was little different from Christianity since then – the same sorts of tensions and differences, even divisions, such as we know all too well today! But from another point of view it is a very liberating, even encouraging conclusion. The first Christians were not stained glass window saints, whose feet rarely touched ground. They were like us! Their churches belonged not to paradise but to the real world. Apart from anything else, this means that what is written to these churches can speak all the more meaningfully and forcibly to us, because it is written to churches like ours!

2. If we draw attention to the diversity of apostolic Christianity we must also note its *unity*. If earliest Christianity was not a uniform phenomenon but more like a spectrum of differing types of Christianity, we must also emphasize what it was which held the spectrum together. What united the first Christians more than anything else was their belief in Jesus – in Jesus as the climax of God's ongoing purpose for man's redemption, the one whom God had raised from the dead and exalted as Lord, the man who demonstrated most clearly what God is like. Clustered round this central distinguishing belief of the first Christians were a number of others on which they would all have agreed in essence, even if their outworking in fuller formulation and practical application diverged in differing degrees: God, the Creator and the Father of Jesus Christ, as one; salvation through faith in Christ; the experience of the Spirit; the Old Testament as scripture and the traditions of Jesus, both to be treasured as authoritative for faith and life; Christianity's continuity with Israel, the people of God; practice of baptism in the name of Jesus and of the Lord's Supper in remembrance of him; and the need for an ethical outworking of faith through love. Such is the heartland of Christianity still.

3. The spectrum held together by these convictions and practices was broader than has often been assumed, but not as broad as some have argued. The ends of the spectrum included beliefs and practices of which the major spokesmen of apostolic Christianity did not approve. Despite this, they did not rush to cut off the ends of the spectrum. On the contrary, the first century was a period in which the leading creative figures (particularly Paul and John) were in effect

pushing out the ends of the spectrum and exploring the boundaries and breadth of Christianity properly so called. Yet, even so, there were those who found the spectrum too constrictive, who could not live within it, and who developed forms and expressions of religious faith and practice which increasingly in the second century were judged to be unacceptable as expressions of that central faith in Christ.

4. Though Catholicism subsequently narrowed the diversity of acceptable Christianity by losing some of the openness and breadth of apostolic Christianity, it nevertheless retained in the New Testament canon a good range of that original diversity. Consequently we have within the source documents of our common faith a powerful self-correcting mechanism. They provide a penetrating criticism of any attempts to force Christianity into a narrower channel or more tightly controlled structure or more consistent form. And they have the potential to spark off renewal which cannot easily be contained within the more restrictive forms of traditional structures. By the grace of God such movements – I think for example of St Francis, the Reformation, John Wesley and twentieth-century Pentecostalism – have often brought renewal to the church as a whole. Where man seeks to control, God seeks to release!

Note on the Gospel of Thomas

Since the claim made in *Jesus: the Evidence*, that Gnostic Christianity was one of the oldest forms of Christianity, was largely based on the Gospel of Thomas, it is probably advisable to say a little more about it.

The Gospel of Thomas, a collection of 114 sayings of varying lengths attributed to Jesus, is the most interesting and most commented on of the Nag Hammadi documents mentioned above (p. 98). It is quite clear that many of the sayings go back to very early memories of Jesus' teaching. About twenty-five per cent of them are paralleled in whole or in part by Q tradition (the tradition which provides a source for much of the Gospels of Matthew and Luke). At the same time there is clear evidence that the sayings have been worked over, elaborated in one or more directions and added to. And again and again the most obvious explanation is that the Gnostic elements belong to the elaborations of the later editions.

In fact we can trace some of the process of elaboration. For we also have some earlier fragmentary papyri found at Oxyrhynchus in Egypt round about the turn of the century. These contain what seem to be one or more *earlier* editions of the Gospel of Thomas. This observation is consistent with the relative datings of the documents, since the papyri date from the end of the second or the first half of the third centuries, while the Gospel of Thomas found at Nag Hammadi was probably written no earlier than the fourth century.

From one of the sayings preserved in both we can begin to gain some idea of how the elaboration proceeded.

Matthew 7.7–8 and 11.28 – ' . . . Seek and you will find; . . . he who seeks finds . . .'. 'Come to me . . . and I will give you rest.'

Pap. Ox. 654.5–9 – '(Jesus says:)
Let him who see(ks) not cease (seeking until) he finds;
and when he finds (he will) be astounded,
and having been (astoun)ded, he will reign;
an(d reigning), he will (re)st.'
(Clement of Alexandria also knows the saying in this form.)

Gospel of Thomas 2 – 'Jesus said:
He who seeks should not stop seeking until he finds;
and when he finds, he will be bewildered (beside himself);
and when he is bewildered, he will marvel,
and will reign over the All.'

'The All' is a regular Gnostic concept, and, as the above comparisons suggest the most obvious explanation is that it was one of the last elements to be added to the saying.

Here then we see a saying whose earliest form can indeed be traced back with firm confidence to the earliest tradition of Jesus' teaching. But we can see too how the saying came to be elaborated and by means of the elaboration given an increasingly Gnostic colouring. In other words, the saying as we now have it in the Nag Hammadi Gospel of Thomas gives no encouragement to the thesis of a form of Gnostic Christianity already existing in the first century. Rather it confirms the counter thesis that the Gnostic element in Gnostic Christianity is a second-century syncretistic outgrowth on the stock of the earlier Christianity. What we can see clearly in the case of this one saying is probably representative of the lengthy process of development and elaboration which resulted in the form of the Gospel of Thomas found at Nag Hammadi.

However justified then the Gnostic Gospel of Thomas may be in claiming that the apostle Thomas was the original source of the sayings preserved in the Gospel of Thomas, it is hard to give much credence to the claim that the Gnostic elements in that collection go back to Thomas himself or to the earliest stages of the Thomas tradition. Consequently the mere fact that the apostle Thomas is linked by ancient tradition with the beginnings of Christianity else-where, namely Edessa, in eastern Syria, hardly provides evidence that the earliest form of Christianity in Edessa was Gnostic. Such a flimsy link can hardly bear anything of the weight put upon it by *Jesus: the Evidence*. By treating the speculation of a few scholars as though it were something more in the nature of an established fact, the programme did no service either to scholarship or to the investigation of how Christianity began.

Concluding Reflections

Christianity has nothing to fear from scholarship! Scholarship is concerned with truth – to discover the reality of things, of people and society, of history and religion. And Christianity is also concerned with truth. It is because Christianity claims to have found in Jesus Christ the key to a true understanding of reality that it speaks so much of that man from a small middle-eastern country nineteen and a half centuries ago. Since Christianity and scholarship share the same passion for truth, Christianity and scholarship are in fact natural allies – common foes of all forms of falsehood, distortion and obscurantism.

So Christianity has nothing to fear from scholarship. Scholars may be a different matter! For individual scholars have their biases and prejudices like every other human being. Individual scholars may see a particular truth only partially or in a fragmentary way or in a distorting light. They may even bend what they see of the truth to serve their own or narrowly party ends. But even so, Christiantiy need have little fear of such scholars. For scholars have to work from the evidence available to them. And evidence has the happy knack of undermining the overblown or unbalanced edifices built upon it. The history of scholarship is littered with the wrecks and tatters of theses and hypotheses and opinions which the evidence subverted or outgrew. Thankfully, scholarship is larger than the opinions of any particular scholar, however eminent.

So Christians have nothing to fear from scholarship and little to fear from particular scholars. On the contrary, they should welcome the critically inquiring and investigative skills of scholars. For since Christians are also concerned with the truth, they should also want to be made aware of and delivered from untruth, in all its forms. If Christians have inherited a too one-sided or overly narrow under-standing of Christianity, they should want to know it. If they have developed a false perspective on any aspect of reality, they should want to know it. If Christianity itself should happen to be false, they should want to know that too. For if Jesus Christ is *not* in fact the key to a true understanding of reality, the sooner they know that the better. So Christians should welcome an open-minded and open-ended inquiry after truth, confident with the confidence of faith that any clarification of the truth, any stripping away of distorting accretions, any correction of misleading perspectives will only strengthen their hold on the truth which is in Christ Jesus.

In such a spirit of inquiry we have looked at four large, but only four, aspects of the beginnings of Christianity. My earnest hope is that these all too brief investigations have illustrated the importance and value of scholarly inquiry to the Christian faith and have helped those who have persevered thus far to recognize that scholarship need not be regarded as the enemy of faith or threatening to devotion. If I were to spell out more fully what seems to me to be the importance of the foregoing for the people of the pew, it would have to be along the following lines.

1. *The importance of recognizing the New Testament documents, Gospels included, for what they are.* The danger is ever present that we make the Gospels what *we* want them to be – that we evaluate them, consciously or unconsciously, by the criteria of modern historiography or modern biography or indeed modern theology. They are none of these. They are what they show themselves to be – Gospels – a quite distinctive type of literature. It was, in fact, these writings which gave us the word ('Gospel') as the title of a book! As 'Gospels' they are concerned to proclaim Jesus. The real Jesus, the Jesus who was and is. There is no flight from history with them, not even with John's Gospel. But neither is there a pedantic concern simply to repeat and pass on earlier forms and formulae as though that was how the gospel of Jesus Christ could adequately be preached. Rather, if we are to speak in generalizations, their concern is to present the heart of the matter, whether the heart of a particular teaching, or of a particular incident, or the heart of the event of Jesus Christ as a whole, and to present it in such a way that each episode as well as the whole reveals the truth of Jesus, the truth of what he said or did on a particular occasion, or the truth that is Jesus himself. The scholarship which recognizes this character of the Gospels thereby frees the Christian student and disciple to accept the Gospels on their own terms, and thereby helps prevent the Christian student and disciple from missing what is central out of overconcern for the peripheral, from failing to see the wood because of the trees, from losing the message in a fruitless debate over the detail.

As a partial parallel, readers may like to consider the relation of this book to the lectures from which the book is derived. The book is not the lectures. They were not tape-recorded or transcribed. But the content is just the same, as anyone who reads the book and recalls the lectures will no doubt confirm. Harder evidence is given by the handouts, varying from one typewritten page to two and a half pages per lecture. That outline, with my own marginal notes used in the

lectures, provided the base or core of the chapters of the book, and
often I have incorporated the wording of the outline with little or no
change. The content is the same, but not the same. For on the one
hand there will be several spontaneous elaborations of particular
points given in the lectures which I have forgotten. And on the other
the exercise of setting down a full text on paper has allowed for a
good deal of elaboration and a degree of literary stylizing which was
neither appropriate nor practical in the lectures. The same, but not
the same. Are they a trustworthy record of what I said in the lectures?
Word for word – No! Sense for sense – assuredly Yes!

2. *The importance of recognizing the inadequacy of human words
to speak adequately of divine reality.* For example, it is no use the
Christian apologist insisting that Jesus has to be seen as the Son of
God in a fully literal sense. Unless we regard God as having a physical
body, and as conceiving Jesus through physical reproduction, we
cannot use 'the Son of God' for Jesus in such a literal sense. The title
is more in the nature of an analogy, or, if you like, a metaphor,
drawn from the everyday world of human conception and birth to
describe a relation which transcends the human and physical. Of
course the metaphor tells us something that is real and true – of a
relationship between God and Jesus which is as close in the divine
(and divine-human) sphere as the father-son relationship can be in
the human sphere. But the correlation between the two uses of the
word 'son' is not a one-to-one correlation.

To put the same point in a slightly different way. We must be
prepared to see some distinction or distance between the *reality*
denoted by phrases like 'son of God' and 'resurrection' and the
phrases themselves. The reality behind these phrases should never be
confused with or reduced to the phrases themselves. Were it possible
to express the same reality more fully in more appropriate terms, we
would not want to remain confined and cramped within that phrase.
And part of a scholar's task is to explore alternative formulations of
such key phrases to see if they do in fact 'fit' or express what we
know of that reality in a more meaningful way – a very necessary
task since the meaning of words and phrases changes from language
to language and from one epoch to another. The fact is that both the
phrases we have instanced ('son of God' and 'resurrection') have
proved themselves particularly appropriate to the task they were
given. Both express a truth about Jesus which other formulations do
not seem to grasp so well. But, nevertheless, it would be a mistake
to focus too much attention on the form and to confuse it with the
reality behind the form. And scholars must be encouraged to pry
behind our language, even our sacred language, to see what the
reality behind it was and is, lest we find one day too late that our

language has become an idol which no longer embodies the truth we should be living by.

3. *The importance of recognizing the diversity within apostolic Christianity, the Christianity of our canonical documents.* The implications of this have not as yet been sufficiently appreciated in their significance for the ecumenical discussions and hopes which have been such a feature of twentieth-century Christianity. For it means that the diversity of the denominations is much more firmly rooted in the New Testament scriptures than has usually been acknowledged. Apostolic Christianity contained a diversity of faith and order which does not fit easily within a single organizational structure. Some at least of the resistance to particular ecumenical schemes has been as deeply grounded in the New Testament as the schemes themselves – perhaps more so! This should give fresh cause for pause at a time when more ambitious hopes of ecumenical coming together in Britain have been stalled once again.

I have no wish whatsoever to backtrack on the ecumenical developments which have taken place. On the contrary, for many years I have wanted to be known simply as a Christian rather than having to own to particular labels. My concern is rather whether the canonical weight given to the necessity (and inevitability) of diversity has been given sufficient weight in our hopes for the coming great church. For one important lesson from the New Testament seems to be, that unless Christians are given room within any particular ecclesiastical structure to express the truth of Christ and of his salvation as they have understood and experienced it, they will simply express it outside that structure. The movement of the Spirit in twentieth-century Pentecostalism is simply a reminder that the Spirit blows where he will. The Spirit creates the church and is not contained by the church. Any church which does not give the Spirit sufficient freedom will simply be bypassed by the Spirit. And since the life of the Spirit comes to diverse expression in different cultures and contexts it is imperative that the church of the future gives scope for that diversity, for that canonical diversity, otherwise that diversity will simply express itself in renewed tension and division. According to Paul, the unity of the body of Christ *depends* on the diversity of its members functioning in their diversity. Without sufficient diversity, the body cannot be one!

4. If all this is so, then an important corollary follows for both faith and order. It is that *my* truth and *my* confession and *my* liturgy can never be *the* truth, *the* confession, *the* liturgy. It is always provisional and approximate and inadequate in relation to the greater reality which human words and actions can never encapsulate or fully express. That must mean that humility is always more appropriate in

such matters than dogmatism. But it also means that *your* truth and *your* confession and *your* liturgy may also be as close to (or as far from) that greater reality, even when it disagrees with mine on what I or you count as important elements of the whole. Humility means not only recognizing when I am less than right, but also recognizing that we *both* may be right in more or less equivalent measure. How dare I hit you over the head with my form of truth. How dare I insist that you mouth my formulae after me. 'Who are you to pass judgment on the servant of another? It is before his own master that he stands or falls. And he will be upheld, for the Master is able to make him stand' (Rom. 14.4).

Speaking personally, one of the most liberating insights which was ever given me by God's grace with regard to subjects on which Christians disagree, was the recognition that in order for *me* to be *right*, it is not necessary for *you* to be *wrong*! An insight which is as true for denominations as it is for individuals. We *all* only 'see in a mirror dimly'. We *all* know only 'in part' (I Cor. 13.12). The full light of God's truth which will swallow up our partial insights and provisional formulations has yet to shine in full strength on our petty and disordered minds. Until then liberty of opinion, genuine respect for those who differ and a reverent agnosticism in many matters of secondary importance is a wholly proper and indeed essential response of faith. Since we walk by faith and not by sight, our confidence should be in the God and Father of our Lord Jesus Christ, rather than in what we can see and handle and control. 'Let him who boasts, boast of the Lord'!

Suggestions for Further Reading

1: The Gospels: Fact, Fiction or What?

R. E. Brown. *The Critical Meaning of the Bible*. Chapman and Paulist Press, 1981.

R. F. Collins. *Introduction to the New Testament*. SCM Press and Doubleday, 1983.

B. Gerhardsson. *The Origins of the Gospel Traditions*. SCM Press and Fortress Press, 1979.

J. H. Hayes and C. R. Holladay. *Biblical Exegesis: A Beginner's Handbook*. SCM Press and John Knox Press, 1983.

G. E. Ladd. *The New Testament and Criticism*. Eerdmans, 1966, and Hodder, 1967.

I. H. Marshall (ed.). *New Testament Interpretation*. Paternoster, 1977, and Eerdmans, 1978.

K. F. Nickle. *The Synoptic Gospels: An Introduction*. SCM Press and John Knox Press, 1982.

J. A. T. Robinson. *Can We Trust the New Testament?* Mowbray, 1977.

2: Did Jesus Claim to Be the Son of God?

J. D. G. Dunn. *Christology in the Making*. SCM Press and Westminster Press, 1980.

M. Hengel. *The Son of God*. SCM Press and Fortress Press, 1976.

A. M. Hunter. *According to John*. SCM Press, 1968, and Westminster Press, 1969.

I. H. Marshall. *The Origins of New Testament Christology*. IVP, 1976, and Eerdmans, 1978.

C. F. D. Moule. *The Origin of Christology*. Cambridge, 1977.

J. Painter. *John: Witness and Theologian*. SPCK, 1975.

J. A. T. Robinson. *The Human Face of God*. SCM Press and Westminster Press, 1973.

S. Smalley. *John—Evangelist and Interpreter*. Paternoster and Attic Press, 1978.

3: What Did the First Christians Believe About the Resurrection?

R. E. Brown. *The Virginal Conception and Bodily Resurrection of Jesus.* Chapman and Paulist-Newman Press, 1973.

J. D G. Dunn. *Jesus and the Spirit.* SCM Press and Westminster Press, 1975, chapter 5.

P. Lapide. *The Resurrection of Jesus.* Augsburg, 1983, and SPCK, 1984.

C. F. D. Moule. *The Significance of the Message of the Resurrection for Faith in Jesus Christ.* SCM Press and Allenson, 1968.

G. O'Collins. *The Easter Jesus.* Darton, Longman & Todd and Judson Press (as *The Resurrection of Jesus Christ*), 1973.

P. Perkins. *Resurrection: New Testament Witness and Contemporary Reflection.* Chapman and Doubleday, 1984.

A. M. Ramsey. *The Resurrection of Christ.* Geoffrey Bles, 1945, and Presbyterian Board, 1946.

U. Wilckens. *Resurrection.* St. Andrew, 1977.

4: Earliest Christianity: One Church or Warring Sects?

R. E. Brown. *The Churches the Apostles Left Behind.* Chapman and Paulist Presss, 1984.

S. Brown. *The Origins of Christianity.* Oxford, 1984.

F. F. Bruce. *Men and Movements in the Primitive Church.* Paternoster, 1979.

G. B. Caird. *The Apostolic Age.* Duckworth and Allenson, 1955.

J. D. G. Dunn. *Unity and Diversity in the New Testament.* SCM Press and Westminster Press, 1977.

E. Pagels. *The Gnostic Gospels.* Weidenfeld & Nicolson and Random House, 1979.

R. L. Wilken. *The Myth of Christian Beginnings.* SCM Press and John Knox Press, 1979.

R. McL. Wilson. *Gnosis and the New Testament.* Blackwell and Fortress Press, 1968.

Other writings by James Dunn of relevance to the issues raised by *Jesus: The Evidence*
"The Messianic Secret in Mark," *Tyndale Bulletin* 21, 1970, pp. 92–117; briefer version in *The Messianic Secret,* ed. C. Tuckett, SPCK and Fortress Press, 1983, pp. 116–131.
"Demythologizing—the Problem of Myth in the New Testament," *New Testament Interpretation: Essays in Principles and Methods,* ed. I. H. Marshall, Paternoster, 1977, and Eerdmans, 1978, pp. 285–307.
(with G. H. Twelftree) "Demon-Possession and Exorcism in the New Testament," *Churchman* 94, 1980, pp. 210–225

"Models of Christian Community in the New Testament," *The Church Is Charismatic: The World Council and the Charismatic Renewal,* ed. A. Bittlinger, WCC, 1981, pp. 99–116; also in *Strange Gifts? A Guide to Charismatic Renewal,* ed. D. Martin and P. Mullen, Blackwell, 1984, pp. 1–18.

"The Authority of Scripture According to Scripture," *Churchman* 96, 1982, pp. 104–122, 201–225.

"Levels of Canonical Authority," *Horizons in Biblical Theology* 4, 1982, pp. 13–60.

"Let John be John—A Gospel for Its Time," *Das Evangelium und die Evangelien,* ed. P. Stuhlmacher, J. C. B. Mohr, 1983, pp. 309–336.

Testing the Foundations: Current Trends in New Testament Study, University of Durham, 1984.

Index of Biblical References